SALMELA | ARCHITECT

SALMELA | ARCHITECT

THOMAS FISHER WITH A PREFACE BY DAVID SALMELA

PHOTOGRAPHS BY PETER BASTIANELLI-KERZE

UNIVERSITY OF MINNESOTA PRESS

Minneapolis • London

Frontispiece: Albrecht Residence, Red Wing, Minnesota

"A Wolf at My Door" copyright 2005 by Jim Brandenburg
All photographs copyright 2005 by Peter Bastianelli-Kerze unless otherwise noted.
Photograph of David Salmela in his office on page x by Kai Salmela
Photographs on pages 52–53 by David Salmela

PUBLISHED BY THE UNIVERSITY OF MINNESOTA PRESS
111 Third Avenue South, Suite 290
Minneapolis, MN 55401-2520
http://www.upress.umn.edu

Book design by Brian Donahue / bedesign, inc.

Printed in China

LIBRARY OF CONGRESS CATALOGING-IN-PUBLICATION DATA

Fisher, Thomas, 1953-
Salmela architect / Thomas Fisher; preface by David Salmela;
photography by Peter Bastianelli-Kerze.
     p. cm.
  ISBN 0-8166-4257-5 (pb : alk. paper)
1. Salmela, David—Criticism and interpretation. 2. Salmela, David—Catalogs. 3. Architecture—
Minnesota—20th century. 4. Architecture—Scandinavia—Influence. I. Salmela, David. II.
Bastianelli-Kerze, Peter. III. Title.
  NA737.S317F57 2005
  728'.092—dc22
                          2004016282

The University of Minnesota is an equal-opportunity educator and employer.

12 11 10 09 08 07 06 05   10 9 8 7 6 5 4 3 2 1

THE UNIVERSITY OF MINNESOTA PRESS gratefully acknowledges financial assistance provided for this book by the Graham Foundation for Advanced Studies in the Fine Arts and from the following institutions and individuals:

AIA Northern Minnesota

Arlin and Marilyn Albrecht

Rex Blake and Kathy Feil

Michael and Betsy Bolen

Mark and Mary Dell Carlson

Meg and Jerry Castle

Nancy Cosgriff

Lori and Brian Gould

Brian Gruis

Roger and Marjorie Hagen

Brad and Kristine Holmes

Rod and Joan Holmes

Paul and Dorothy Lutz

David and Kathy Matthew

Edward and Camille Penhoet

Carl J. Remick Jr.

Jeanne and Scott Wallace

Robert and Joan Wilson

CONTENTS

DAVID SALMELA

The design process I follow is difficult to explain. Architecture is complicated, entailing many issues and many players and having a long-lasting impact. Good architecture needs to resolve all programs for all users of a place with simplicity, beauty, and comfort. Each project is like chess: complex, with every game being different. A project may start the same (if you start first), but every subsequent move is a reaction, intuitive as well as structured. At the end there is a solution that, if built, will be viewed by all who pass by until it is taken down.

The three most crucial issues of architecture today are not about design direction but rather the preservation and sensitive use of the natural environment, the preservation and sensitive use of our existing built environment, and the sensitivity of design within the context of the first two. Architectural design has limitless, meaningful references and inspiration just waiting to be noticed regionally, nationally, and internationally.

I was raised on a farm in a predominantly Finnish community in central Minnesota. It wasn't difficult, even at a young age, to recognize that farming and building altered the natural environment. It was also obvious that some of the farms were remarkably beautiful: how the fields were cut, the rows of trees planted for windbreak, the buildings placed in an order of function—how the materials and colors, the orchards and gardens and lawns created a unique pastoral setting. I learned that tilled land and built buildings can be attractive; if they are thought out thoroughly and given great effort, the worth of these structures would be evident. This simple understanding is also the basis of comprehending design and leads to appreciation of the more complex areas that affect good design: the cultures of regions, the regions of countries, the countries of the continent, and so on. Universal ideas of architectural design apply to all but are never applied the same way in each place.

Eino Jyring, a Finnish American architect, and his partner, Richard Whiteman, were the first to give me a position in 1969 in the architectural firm Aguar, Jyring, Whiteman, and Moser in Hibbing, Minnesota. One year later I moved to John Damberg's firm, then Damberg and Peck, in Virginia, Minnesota, where I worked for twenty years. In 1989, Dale Mulfinger of Mulfinger Susanka in Minneapolis gave me the opportunity to head a branch office in Duluth, where one year later Salmela Fosdick, Ltd., was established. In 1994 I became sole proprietor and formed Salmela Architect. Since 2000 the talented Souliyahn Keobounpheng has worked for me. I also work closely with the creative structural engineer Bruno Franck, an associate professor in the College of Architecture and Landscape Architecture at the University of Minnesota–Twin Cities. My recent projects have included the skilled services of Shane Coen and Jon Stumpf of Coen + Stumpf and Associates (since 2000, Coen + Partners). This association between architect and landscape architect has greatly raised the quality of the finished project.

Since the mid-1980s the firm of Rod and Sons Carpentry has built fourteen of my projects. Rod Holmes, father and founder, headed the first two projects. Brothers Brad and Curt Holmes have carried on their father's tradition of the highest-quality craftsmanship. Brad's talent as an expediter, carpenter, and cabinetmaker has allowed for the accomplishment of more daring concepts than one would typically attempt.

Peter McKinnon of River City Builders has collaborated with me on three substantial projects and is another quality-oriented contractor with whom I have been fortunate to work.

Harold Teasdale, the developer who stayed the course on the Jackson Meadow project, is a rare person in his openness to ideas not typically practiced in his field. We continue to work on this major endeavor.

The longest relationship I have shared in my career has been with Peter Bastianelli-Kerze. Since the 1970s he and I have worked together to capture the feel of my projects on film. I am indebted to his amazing eye for the essence of each project and his untiring efforts to record the total statement. Without Peter's images these projects would be less understood.

Jim Brandenburg's talents span beyond photography and his reputation to the world. As a client he was the ultimate. I thank him for his time to record our experience.

This book is dedicated to my wife, Gladys; my children, Cory, Chad, Tia, Kai, and Brit; and all of the clients with whom I have been so fortunate to work.

Duluth, Minnesota

March 2005

WILSON RESIDENCE, LAKE VERMILION, TOWER, MINNESOTA

EMBRACING OPPOSITES

When you visit David Salmela's office, you enter a world firmly rooted in Minnesota's north woods, where legends of giants, elves, and trolls still hold. High on a hill above Lake Superior, amid the faint whiff of pine, the office occupies a back wing added to Salmela's two-story house on a street of equally modest residences. When you approach the house, the only indication of the office is a white-painted, wide-board fence, at once oversized and lighthearted. Running along the side property line, its undulating height draws you to the back and screens the narrow boardwalk and office entry from the neighboring house.

That sense of playfulness and unexpected scale continues when Salmela greets you at the office door. His broad smile, firm handshake, and effusive personality sparkling behind round, black glasses give his small frame an oversized presence. Just inside the door, an unusually narrow stair with high walls, lined with the framed design awards Salmela has won for his work over the years, leads to a small drafting room above. The first-floor office has a nearly bare inner room, with a small conference table, bookshelves, file cabinets, and copy machine, opening to a tidy but crowded work space off the back of the house, with a center desk and low shelves of magazines and a drafting table flooded with natural light from the room's oversized windows.

On almost every available surface, small, gray chipboard models abound. Like the workroom of a wizard, this space looks as if it were also inhabited by some tiny race of people, occupying the many houses whose shapes—hollow prism roofs, linked repetitive gables, oddly angled windows—have both a strangeness and familiarity. You feel like a giant amid all of those small cardboard models, and at the same time you feel like a child, wanting to play with them. Such extremes—large and small, work and play—are not just happenstance. They offer a key insight into Salmela's architecture, and the very reason why it rewards careful scrutiny.

Blaise Pascal, the seventeenth-century thinker, once wrote, "A man does not show his greatness by being at one extremity, but rather by touching both at once." The greatness of Salmela's work lies in precisely that. He pursues not one extreme or another, seeking neither the avant-garde nor tradition. Instead, he touches aspects of both extremes at the same time, showing us a way out of the one-sided extremism that has handicapped much of the architecture of our time.

The arts today thrive on such extremes: on the outrageous act and tortured vision on one hand or on oppressive order and superficial ornament on the other. We too often have to choose between sublime subversiveness and banal beauty in our arts as well as in our public life. And if we try to take a stand against either extreme, we find ourselves attacked from both sides or simply dismissed as mediocre. Being in the middle brings charges of being middling.

But Pascal, a brilliant mathematician and a theologian, had something else in mind. He knew all too well that one extreme informs the other; indeed, that one extreme cannot exist without the other. He also knew that embracing both at once is not the easiest path but the hardest of all, since it demands balancing that which resists balance.

Such is the difficulty—and value—of what David Salmela has achieved, both in his work and in his career. He has become one of the most awarded architects in Minnesota, with twenty-eight state and national design awards in the seventeen years between 1987 and 2004, yet he never attended architecture school, having become licensed at a time when work experience—in his case, with engineers, builders, and architects—could substitute for formal education in the field. He has achieved international prominence, having been published more than one hundred times in European as well as American books, magazines, and newspapers over the same period, yet he practices at the fringe of the architectural community, in Duluth, Minnesota, a charming but relatively small and somewhat isolated industrial city at the west end of Lake Superior. And he has created a consistent body of remarkable buildings, all of them challenging in their ideas, yet he has done so in projects as small as a stand-alone sauna, as modest as a storage building, and as constrained as developer housing.

He has shown, in other words, that great work can happen anywhere, on any budget, with the simplest of programs. It demands only that you simultaneously embrace the opposite extreme: believing, as Salmela has, that every project offers an opportunity to explore an idea, to make a larger connection.

FRAMED BY A PLAYFULLY DESIGNED FENCE, DAVID SALMELA'S STUDIO SITS AT THE BACK OF HIS HOUSE IN DULUTH, MINNESOTA.

This embrace of opposites also occurs in the way Salmela designs and builds his architecture. Almost all of his buildings have been newly constructed, yet many have used the timber of old buildings, available from a salvage yard near Duluth. And while his buildings engage the material realm, Salmela's work also shows how relationships between people and connections to a place—the social and spiritual realms—can make all the difference between great work and that which isn't. For example, the Holmeses—a contractor family who has been a client of Salmela's—have constructed many of his buildings, and Peter Kerze—also a client—has photographed most of them.

Salmela draws from the work of other architects, and his buildings have superficial resemblances to other modern and postmodern structures. However, his mode of operation differs from that of other architects and that makes all the difference.

Alvar Aalto, the great Finnish modern architect, looms perhaps largest as an influence on Salmela, understandable given both their shared ethnic origin as well as the similarities in the climate and topography of Minnesota and Finland. Early Salmela work, such as the Webster house, with its asymmetrical shed roofs, stepped windows, vertical board cladding, and dividable interior, recalls Aalto's Villa Kokkonen, while the white-slat room dividers and window screens in Salmela's Emerson and Albrecht houses echo a common feature of Aalto's buildings, evident in projects such as his Seinajoki City Library or Mount Angel Library. These references to Aalto do more than pay architectural homage. In Salmela's hands, they become ways of simultaneously achieving opposite goals: privacy and views, openness and closure, surface and void. Those goals mean so much to Salmela that in one project, when a client resisted adding a vertical slat screen to a prominent window, the architect offered to resign.

Aldo Rossi influences Salmela's architecture much differently. If Aalto provides ethnic and environmental connections, Rossi provides a rational one, appealing to Salmela's liking of simplicity and directness. The houses of Jackson Meadow, with their evocation of the white-painted, metal-roofed, nineteenth-century houses of the adjacent town,

Marine on St. Croix, bring to mind Rossi's argument that architecture should reflect the particular history and quality of a place. The spare form, repetitive order, and symmetrical organization of the houses and outbuildings at Jackson Meadow also reflect Rossi's rationalism. Yet there is an irrational streak in Salmela's interpretation of Rossi's repetitions. At Jackson Meadow, garages have not one gable roof but six, and houses have not one front door but twelve.

Postmodern influences abound in Salmela's work as well. The oversized and undersized windows of Robert Venturi's mother's house, the layers of screen walls in Charles Moore's architecture, the exposed studs of Frank Gehry's early work—all find their way into Salmela's projects. The wood-stud screen porches of his Wilson and Albrecht houses seem like Gehry structures shorn of their cladding. The flat ornament at Salmela's Unger-Sonnerup house and the illusion of depth in the façade of his Kerze house recall the play of scales in Moore's buildings. And the range of window sizes in Salmela's Wild Rice Restaurant and of window types in the Loken house look to the exaggerations of Venturi.

If architectural influences echo in Salmela's work, so do vernacular ones. He refers to the decorated formality of Swedish villas in the Unger-Sonnerup house, to the colorful plainness of Finnish farmhouses in the Smith house, and to the rambling diversity of American farmsteads in the Jones house. In all of these projects, he gives a nod to history, but with a wink of the eye. The Swedish symbolism in the Unger-Sonnerup house gets flattened and abstracted in modern fashion. The interior of the Smith farmhouse has a "free" plan right out of Mies van der Rohe. And the Jones farmstead surprises you with a glass pavilion enclosing the main rooms.

There are qualities of Salmela's architecture that seem beyond influence, that draw from a deeper, imaginative vision all his own. The Brandenburg house and studio, for instance, alludes to modernist and vernacular architecture, but it also seems to have arisen out of a Scandinavian myth: a settlement that Viking invaders might have built had they ventured inland to settle among the Native Americans.

Similar narratives, at once ancient and modern, underlie other Salmela projects. The Emerson sauna looks like a house sized for Munchkins, with a roof seeming displaced by a tornado not unlike the one that brought Dorothy to Oz. The Albrecht house also possesses a mythic character. Its rooftop office and porch stand like a small Acropolis on the brick base of the house, inviting us to find our way to it, and from it to look out over the Mississippi River that is our Nile.

And on and on it goes, in one Salmela project after another: the Thompson house repeating the chronology of Scandinavian settlement in America across its façade, the Loken stable recalling a time when farm buildings hunched and sagged like the animals they housed, the Gooseberry Falls State Park Visitors Center reminding us of the ancient trees and rocks and soil from which the building sprang. In almost all of the work shown here, Salmela draws from deep cultural roots to create an architecture that, while particular to its place and people, ends up having a universal appeal.

The work has an intellectual appeal as well. David Salmela pursues in his buildings—sometimes consciously, sometimes not—a range of provocative and often witty ideas. Many of these ideas raise questions about our relationship to the natural world and about the relationship of elements within nature itself.

The Carlson house and outbuildings, for example, suggest one way of sensitizing us to the balance of nature by helping us see the symmetry of architectural form as an analog to the symmetry of the natural world. The Holmes house suggests another way, revealing how buildings follow the same principles of adaptation and complexity that underlie nature. Meanwhile, Salmela uses architectural means in the Gooseberry Falls park pavilion to connect us to the four elements—earth, air, fire, and water—while in the expansion and contraction of the Webster house he shows how the change of seasons can awaken us to nature's flux over time.

Salmela's work also suggests that how we relate to nature depends on how we conceive of it. At the Hanson house, nature exists not as something apart from us or something that we can exploit, but as an extension of human nature, with all of the same rights that accrue to us. In a different vein, the Brandenburg house and studio expresses, in architectural form, an idea of evolution that is not linear and continuous but nonlinear and punctuated, full of leaps forward and back.

How we might live more sustainably also depends on our seeing human communities as extensions of nature. At Jackson Meadow, Salmela, along with landscape architects Shane Coen and Jon Stumpf, has created a community in which the majority of the land remains in its natural state, with the housing tightly clustered or carefully fitted to the topography. Meanwhile, in the Unger-Sonnerup house, Salmela reminds us of a premodern answer to the sustainability question: treating nature as an arcadia, within which the utopian virtues of self-restraint and self-sacrifice flourish.

Questions of our relationship to nature lead, in Salmela's work, to other questions pertaining to how we structure the world in which we live. That partly involves thought itself, our ideas and concepts, all of which are simple and yet potentially profound in their implications. In the Wick house, for instance, Salmela plays off the way we structure our day into living and working, interweaving them functionally and formally. And at the Loken house, he derives some of its form from the difference between buildings and bodies while revealing the parallels they share.

We see these connections through the use of conceptual tools. One such tool, evident in the Emerson house and sauna, involves the use of analogies to generate form, both from within architecture as well as from without. Another tool, apparent in the Albrecht house, involves the distinction between truth and falsity when we must decide between the many choices we face in our lives.

We make those distinctions and draw those analogies based on even more fundamental concepts. In the Wild Rice Restaurant, Salmela looks at the sameness or difference among things to help us understand them, while in the Smith house he arranges elements into wholes and parts of larger wholes to do the same. And in the Jones house, he locates things in space and time, both of which can vary in relation to each other to show the connections among them. Architecture not only depends on these fundamental categories of thought, but also makes them real to us.

Architecture also engages ideas inherent to itself, ideas specific to the making of form and the creation of space. Salmela pursues a variety of such ideas in his work.

In the Kerze house and sauna, he plays on the difference between reality and illusion, between facts and the images we create of them. He takes a somewhat different tack in the Thompson house. There, he compares facts and fiction, exploring the difference between the function of a building and the story we tell about it. Another, related idea—the relation of what we see to what we don't see in a building—appears in the Koehler house, where the framing of the structure also frames the various views of the surrounding landscape.

Ideas from arts even fairly far removed from architecture can influence it. In the Lutz house, Salmela performs a visual and spatial riff on the idea of jazz for the home of musicians, with syncopated windows and seemingly improvised forms. And, at the Wilson house, he displays the fragmented reality of our media-dominated world, where choice in the variety of materials and shapes matters more than consistency.

The range of ideas Salmela raises through his work touches extremes quite different from those that have become dominant in the practice of architecture today. So many of the architects whose buildings get widely published operate at a national and international scale, producing one project after another in an often idiosyncratic and highly personal style. As a result, much of their work has an extreme geographical spread but also an extremely narrow range of ideas that get repeated, in slightly different ways, over and over.

Salmela embraces the opposite set of extremes. He works mostly in a narrow geographical area, Minnesota and northern Wisconsin, with only the occasional far-flung project, usually for a client with some connection to his north-woods base. At the same time, he employs a relatively narrow range of forms in his architecture, recalling either the simple, gable-roofed forms of Scandinavian vernacular or the plain, flat-roofed forms of modern architects who have worked at the geographical margins, such as Alvar Aalto or Alvaro Siza.

The plans of Salmela's buildings have an equally narrow range. He often aggregates square bays into long, rectangular rooms containing several functions separated by service elements such as stairs and fireplaces, and he uses these bars of buildings as well as landscape features such as wood fences or stone walls to define intimate outdoor rooms, like those found in a farmstead or village.

But by restricting the geographical and formal aspects of his work, Salmela gives himself the room to explore a wide range of ideas about the context and content of architecture. These ideas emerge not from some highly worked-out theory that he then applies to his buildings, but from a process more akin to a form of play. As in a game, he imposes strict rules on himself, within which he then pushes the limits of what is possible. He also accepts many of the rules that traditions, conventions, and regulations place on him, knowing that to rewrite too many of the rules, as the architectural avant-garde has tried to do over the past century, results in too few wanting to play. Instead, Salmela draws you in, with forms that seem common, even comforting, and then he plays on your expectations, shifting your perspective and undermining your unquestioned assumptions.

The result is a rich mix of the familiar and the strange. Salmela does not try to make the initially strange become familiar, as so many modernists have done, nor does he accept the familiar as *almost* all right, as so many postmodernists have done. Instead, he uncovers the underlying strangeness that exists within the already familiar, creating an unexpected architecture out of the most modest utilitarian structure or the most ordinary house commission.

At a time when the discipline of architecture itself seems uncertain of the next route to take, when postmodernism seems like a dead-end and a return to modernism, like so much backtracking, David Salmela's work offers us another road. That road is much less traveled, located somewhere between magic realism and surrealism. But that road can lead to great work, as you will see on the following pages, work that manages to be both intellectually challenging and publicly engaging, two extremes that in recent decades architecture has touched all too rarely.

GOOSEBERRY FALLS STATE PARK VISITORS CENTER, TWO HARBORS, MINNESOTA

QUANTUM EVOLUTION

SINCE DARWIN, we have become accustomed to thinking of nature as continuous evolution over long periods of time. The more scientists study the natural world, however, the more they find in it stretches of rapid change and unexpected discontinuity, with species moving from one ancestral state to another in relatively small areas and over short time spans. Referring to similar jumps among the smallest particles in nature, scientists have called this "quantum evolution." The house and studio David Salmela designed for famed nature photographer Jim Brandenburg and his family suggests that the same quantum evolution can occur in architecture—the environment in which human nature evolves.

As you approach the cluster of buildings that comprise this house and studio, you feel as if you have come upon a place of uncertain date. The elegant, tall structure to the left of the entry drive, with its large, horizontal band of windows, seems completely modern. But other structures to the left and right of the drive—some with sod roofs, some built of massive logs, all at odd angles to each other—make this complex appear as if it contains buildings from several different time periods, some of them quite old. You feel as if you have stumbled upon an ancient Scandinavian village, forgotten deep in Minnesota's north woods, as if the past had taken a quantum leap forward into the present.

The main house visibly displays this leap. It began as a vacation lodge whose exposed logs, steep gable roof, and broad overhangs protected the building during the long Minnesota winters. When he greatly expanded it for the Brandenburgs, Salmela decided to retain the integrity of the log house and add buildings of similar scale and character, evolving it into a complex of structures—house and studio, garage, workshop, storage and utility buildings set on a level piece of ground overlooking a stream and waterfall.

The additions take their cues from the original log structure. The studio wing to the south has a gable roof that appears to telescope out from that of the lodge, as if the new had evolved in three stages from the old. A low sod-roofed structure, containing living and dining spaces, connects the studio to the log building, housing a new kitchen. Under the studio's gable roof, Salmela has inserted an office and sleeping spaces, and under the lodge's roof, a master bedroom suite. Bands of different-sized windows throughout the house and studio provide various views of the stream below and the wooded hillsides around the house. Like the photography developed here, the structure frames and crops your perception of nature, in all of its evolved diversity.

To the east, across the entry court from the main house, stands another steeply gabled building that contains work space and storage, with a low sod-roofed garage, partly buried into the hill, adjoined to it. Those structures bend around the auto court and gesture to the main house, creating a protected, intimately scaled space, welcome in the seemingly limitless forest that surrounds the complex. On the north side of the main house, an entry deck connects it to another log building, with an exterior stair that leads to a log sauna overlooking the pool at the bottom of the waterfall. It all seems like a slice of Shangri-la, having somehow escaped time.

Similar juxtapositions occur inside the house. Rough-hewn logs and a stone fireplace contrast with smoothly finished wood and thin steel stairs and railings. And small, deeply set or multipaned windows contrast with large sheets of glass, as if the house has undergone alterations over many generations, punctuated by major advances in technology.

When I visited the house, David Salmela, Jim Brandenburg, and I sat on the long bench outside the workroom and talked about the question of photographic "truth," now that computers can seamlessly insert into any photograph an image from a radically different location. Photography, in other words, is undergoing its own quantum evolution, jumping from its traditional role as the most "truth-telling" of the visual arts to one in which differences of space or time can coexist. It's as if we have begun to replicate, through technology, the sudden leaps that we now find throughout nature.

TOP: THE COMPOUND APPEARS BOTH MODERN AND ARCHAIC, EVOKING AN UNCERTAIN POINT IN TIME. **MIDDLE:** ROOFS OF WOOD SHINGLE, BOARD, AND CLAPBOARD EXPRESS THE DIFFERENT PARTS OF THE HOUSE. **BOTTOM:** ADDITIONS ENVELOP AND DEFER TO THE ORIGINAL LOG HOUSE.

This issue lies at the heart of the controversy over "design" and the natural world: has nature evolved through chance or has it been designed? The Brandenburg house, and the photography that emerges from Jim Brandenburg's studio, suggests that we may be making a false distinction by asking the question in that way. Design always involves chance, just as chance occurrences, in hindsight, can seem

TOP: JIM BRANDENBURG'S PHOTOGRAPHY STUDIO IN THE FOREGROUND PROVIDES SEASONAL VIEWS OF THE WOODS AND WILDLIFE. **BOTTOM:** THE HOUSE OVERLOOKS A WATERFALL, WHILE STEPS LEAD TO A SAUNA NEXT TO THE POOL.

designed. Both design and evolution endure sudden leaps, unexpected change, and quantum jumps, and we don't fully understand why such jumps occur in subatomic particles, in natural selection, or in design. And so, like the careful serendipity of the Brandenburg house, the answer to the question of whether nature has evolved through chance or through design might be both, since they are one and the same.

TOP: COMPLETE WITH A BENCH FOR VIEWING, THE AUTO COURT DOUBLES AS A PEDESTRIAN SPACE. **BOTTOM:** BRANDENBURG'S HOUSE AND STUDIO OCCUPY A FORESTED SITE BY A STREAM, WATERFALL, AND POND.

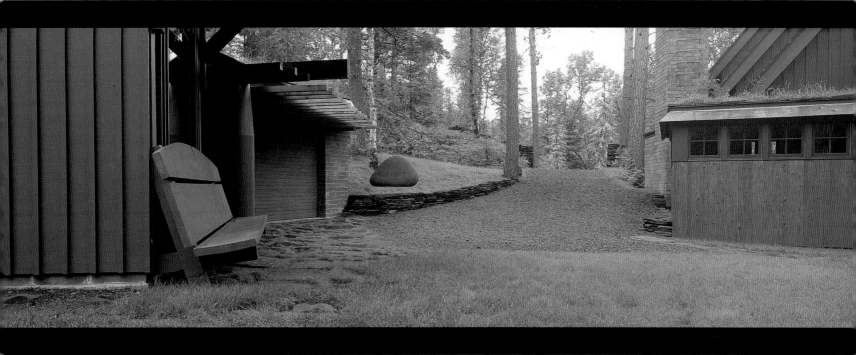

A WOLF AT MY DOOR

JIM BRANDENBURG

WE CALL OUR HOME RAVENWOOD. It began as a quaint log cabin nested atop a waterfall on Uncle Judd's Creek, just outside the border of the three-million-acre Boundary Waters Canoe Area Wilderness. It was hard to imagine the extent to which David Salmela would one day transform this quiet, unassuming structure into a dignified and attention-grabbing composition.

During the early stages, we discussed concept, context, and construction details. Ideas that seemed radical, if not impractical, at the time have become some of our most cherished elements. The sod roofs are evolving ecosystems with grasses and flowers that continually change their seating arrangements; the introduced species are gradually taken over by the native plants, and one day they will finally agree on who gets the best seat and settle into a stable community. The white cedars that were small saplings now thrive in the full sun on the roof and need to be trimmed. My little prairie would become a miniature woods if it weren't attended to. I look through windows into a scene that has revealed to me and my camera some of the deepest secrets in the north woods. The skeptical wolf pack that inhabits the surrounding forest may yet accept me as a neighbor if I behave myself.

It is both an honor and intimidating to live in a home that has received so many accolades. Partly out of respect for David's work and recognizing the possibility that an architecturally minded treasure hunter might drop in for an unannounced visit, I feel prompted to continually tweak, straighten, or rearrange the furnishings—and I do admit to enjoying this ritual. It is exhilarating and exhausting living with this gifted child. My home is demanding. It always needs to be played with, and I often find it difficult to concentrate on my work while surrounded by this wonderful and complex companion.

A home can take on a personality. Sometimes when I am home alone at night, I feel an elusive presence in the air, lonesome and forlorn. Ravenwood is a living organism to me, and the anthropomorphic references are based on real experiences. I will on occasion walk naked through the rooms to get a more intimate feel of the space, like a skinny-dip in a secret pond that brings one closer to nature. The nature lover in me takes this relationship to the extreme, and I envision a time when this grand and majestic land that lured me here will reclaim the bones of my friend. Then the lovely little waterfall I so rudely imposed myself upon will again become the private playground for the otters in this enchanted boreal forest that has taken such good care of me.

OPPOSITE: A CONTINUOUS TABLE IN THE OFFICE OFFERS VIEWS OUT THE CLERESTORY WINDOWS. **LEFT:** AN ENTRY CORRIDOR EXPANDS TO FORM DINING, SITTING, AND VIEWING ALCOVES. **RIGHT:** THE ORIGINAL LOG HOUSE, PAINTED WHITE ON THE INTERIOR, ENCLOSES THE KITCHEN AND BEDROOM.

LEFT: BRANDENBURG'S PHOTOGRAPHY STUDIO AND ITS OFFICE LOFT LOOK OUT OVER THE WOODS. **ABOVE:** HIGH WINDOWS ALONG THE DRIVE LET IN SOUTHERN LIGHT WHILE PROVIDING PRIVACY.

ABOVE: THE GUEST ROOM HAS A PAIR OF BEDS, WITH A STAIR BEYOND LEADING TO AN ADDITIONAL SLEEPING LOFT.

OPPOSITE: A STAIR LEADS UP TO THE GUEST BEDROOM FROM THE ENTRY AREA.

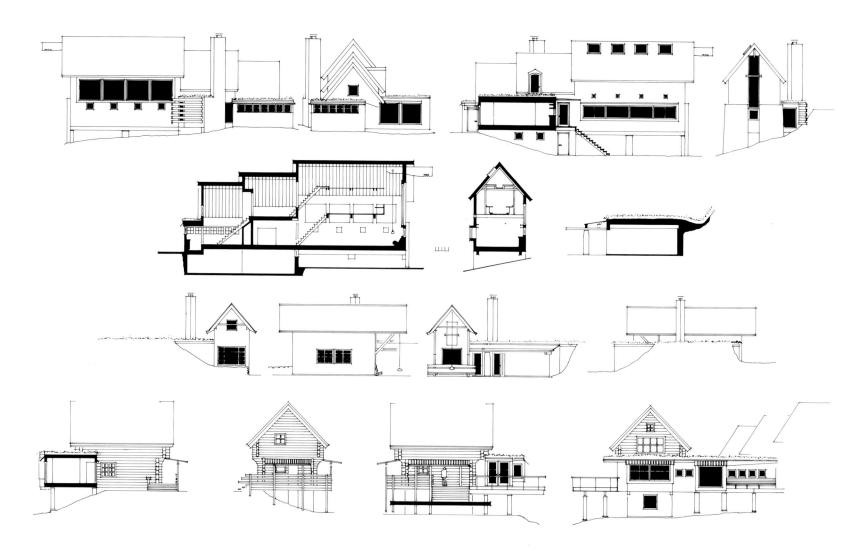

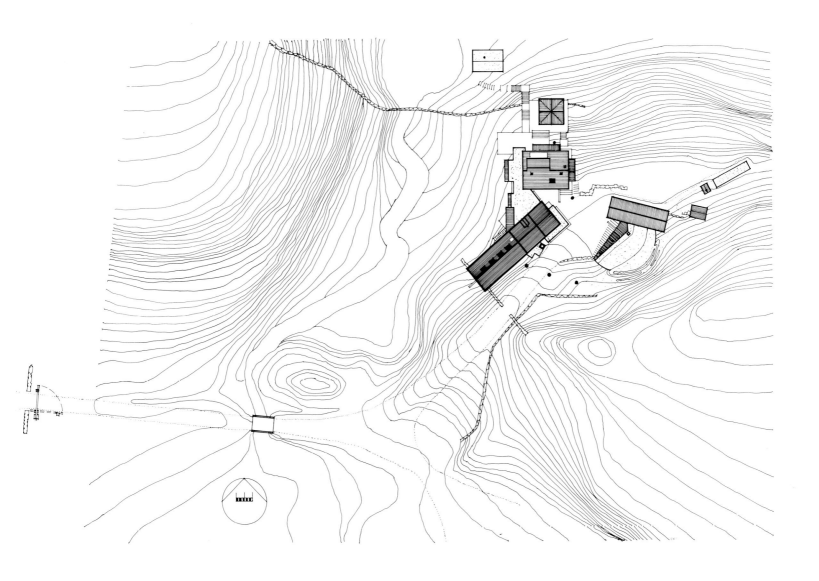

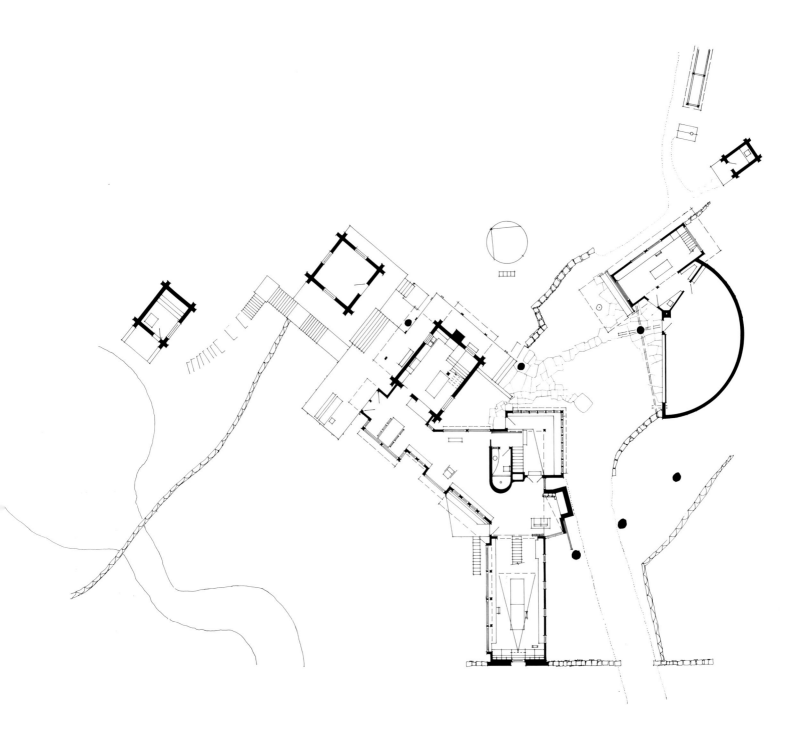

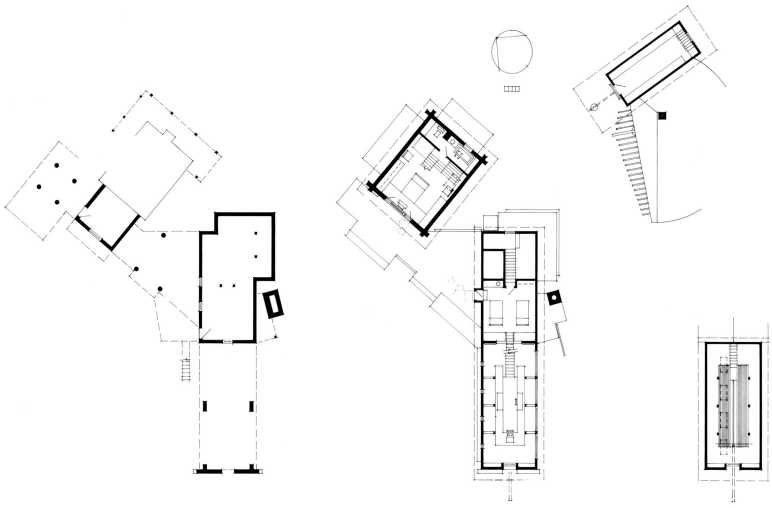
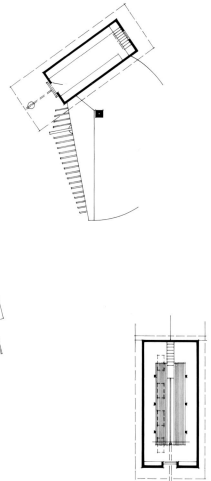

WITHIN AND WITHOUT

DAVID GRUDIN, in his book *The Grace of Great Things: Creativity and Innovation,* observes that creativity often occurs through the use of analogy, which he sees taking two forms: "interdisciplinary" analogies that seek parallels to ideas in other fields, and "intradisciplinary" analogies that take ideas from within a field, altering them to fit new circumstances.

Vernacular architecture has long been intradisciplinary, evolving incrementally over time. Its practitioners select from and often slightly alter building forms and materials from the past. It is architecture that draws analogies to itself. Most modern architecture, however, has been interdisciplinary, finding parallels in other fields—the mechanistic analogy of Le Corbusier's "house-as-a-machine-to-live-in," the biological analogies of Frank Lloyd Wright's "organic" architecture, and even the linguistic analogies of Peter Eisenman's "deconstructivist" projects. The abstractness and revolutionary character of modernism comes from this taking of methods and ideas from entirely different disciplines.

David Salmela's work embraces both strategies at the same time. Rather than seek analogies either within architecture or outside of it, he often creates dialogues between the intra- and the interdisciplinary, between the vernacular and modernism. The Emerson house and sauna offer an example of this. Each structure begins with a different type of analogy and then moves toward the other, resulting in an ensemble of buildings that achieves a kind of unity out of their contrasts.

The house draws an analogy to earlier architecture, to the traditional Scandinavian farmhouse. Consisting of two offset, parallel wings connected by an entry block, the house has steeply gabled roofs, broad overhangs, white walls, and treelike columns that recall the vernacular architecture of the Nordic countries. The analogy has a temporal as well as spatial quality. By varying the floor levels and rooflines of the house, the sizes and shapes of the windows, and the texture and pattern of the siding, Salmela creates what looks like a collection of attached buildings that have emerged over time.

The house also alludes to another architectural analogy: that of the fairy-tale house in the forest. Approached through deep woods, the Emerson house, while large in size, appears small in scale. The north-facing garage and service wing has low eaves and small square windows along its length, making it seem diminutive. Meanwhile, the large square window at the gable end of the main living wing and the even larger square dormer window above the entrance give the house a fantasy quality, reminding us of the experience we all shared as children, when everything seemed bigger, grander.

The third analogy from inside architecture derives from the work of Alvar Aalto. The white wood-slat screen at the entryway that lets in light but not a view; the angled white-brick chimney that seems to walk up the roof; the flowing interior living space flooded with light from the glassy south façade—all of these recall Aalto's idiosyncratic take on modern architecture. He drew heavily, especially in the houses he designed, from Finnish vernacular housing, and Salmela's references to Aalto's work become a kind of reference to traditional buildings once removed.

Yet Aalto also made nonarchitectural analogies in his work; their splayed, angled, and jagged forms recalled those of the landscape, as his architecture became like nature. The Emerson house echoes that in the way the two main wings of the house slide past each other, along different contour lines, with the perpendicular porch that juts into the lawn, like the dock into the nearby lake. The house recapitulates the site.

The newer sauna near the house does something quite different. While it refers to traditional architecture from the side, with its tall gable roof and multi-windowed enclosure, the sauna jolts our expectations, with the gable roof looking as if it had slid mostly off of its brick base, exposing the chimney at its center. The semicircular outdoor shower looks like a prop put in place to keep the roof from falling off completely. The sauna seems like a structure hit by a tornado, making an analogy to nature of a different sort.

TOP: THE SERIES OF GLASS DOORS LINING THE EMERSON HOUSE OPEN TO THE EXPANSIVE LAWN. **MIDDLE:** A SUNKEN ENTRY COURT LEADS TO A RECESSED ENTRY DIVIDED BY A HUGE, TREELIKE COLUMN. **BOTTOM:** THE BACK OF THE HOUSE NEARLY MIRRORS THE ENTRY WITH ANOTHER CENTRAL COLUMN AND DORMER.

ABOVE: THE LIVING ROOM HAS A CENTRAL TELEVISION AND A FIREPLACE SKEWED TO ONE SIDE. **BELOW:** A CURVED CEILING EVOKING A BOAT HULL DEFINES THE BREAKFAST ROOM, WHICH FACES THE LAKE. **OPPOSITE:** THE MASTER BEDROOM SHARES THE LOFTY SPACE OF THE LIVING ROOM, LIGHTED BY HIGH DORMERS.

From the end, the sauna also looks like a geometrical abstraction of a house. The gable roof appears as a triangular prism on its side, with no end walls or interior trusses to interrupt the purity of its shape, a structural feat achieved by engineer Bruno Franck. Likewise, the semicircular shower at one end and the windowless brick box at the other have a geometric clarity that makes the whole outbuilding look like a mathematical exercise in Platonic form.

Yet, as in the house, the sauna begins with one type of analogy and moves toward the other. However much this tiny outbuilding refers to geometry or nature, it also draws an analogy to architecture, especially the rationalist work of Aldo Rossi, whose simple geometrical buildings had an elemental quality analogous to the somewhat primeval character of a sauna deep in the forest, by a pristine lake.

In the end, the analogy that might best fit the Emerson house and sauna is that of conversation, as the two buildings refer to and diverge from each other. The house starts with familiar architectural forms and subtly abstracts them, while the sauna starts with elemental geometrical shapes and slyly renders them architecture. Either approach to analogy works, but as this house and sauna show, the embrace of both works even better, creating a rich dialogue in what David Grudin calls "the grace of great things."

TOP: THE KITCHEN CONSISTS OF GLASS-FACED CUPBOARDS THAT ECHO THE FENESTRATION OF THE HOUSE.
LEFT: A SMALL STAIR, SEPARATED BY SLATS FROM THE ENTRY HALL, LEADS TO TWO UPSTAIRS BEDROOMS.

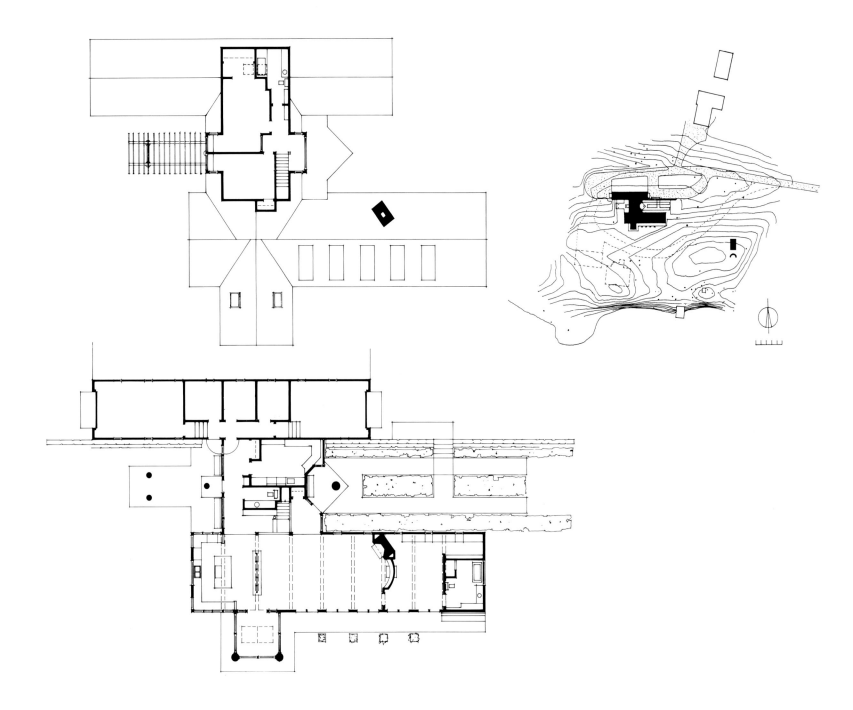

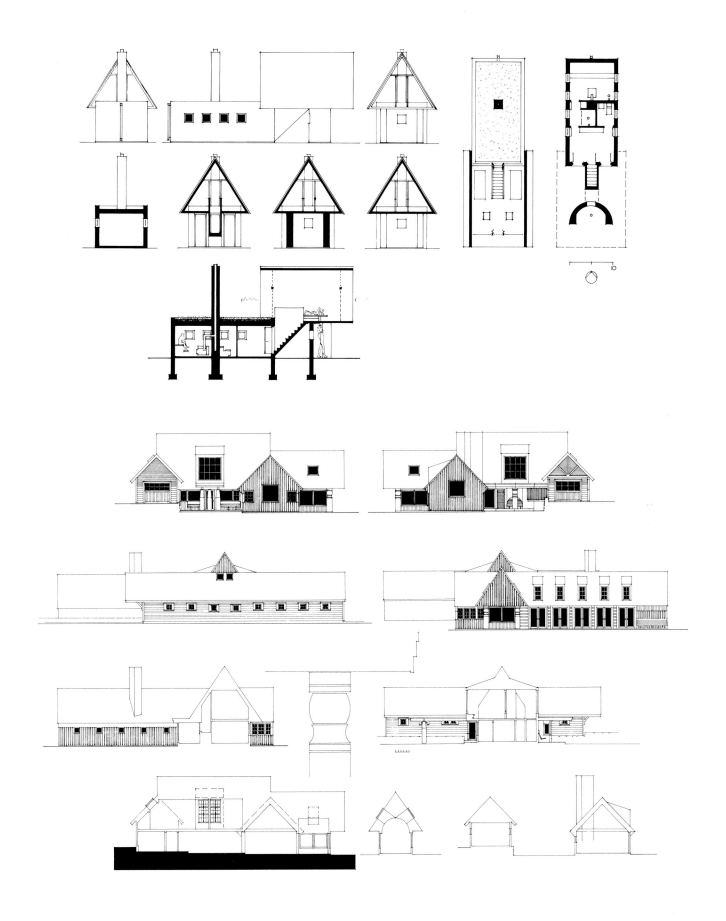

ABOVE: THE MORE RECENT SAUNA SHOWS HOW SALMELA'S ARCHITECTURE HAS BECOME INCREASINGLY ABSTRACT. **BELOW:** THE BACK OF THE SAUNA, WITH ITS GRASS ROOF, LOOKS AS IF IT AROSE OUT OF THE LAWN. **BOTTOM LEFT:** THE SAUNA'S GABLE ROOF LOOKS AS IF IT SLID OFF ITS BRICK BASE, EXPOSING THE CHIMNEY. **MIDDLE LEFT:** A RACK THAT MIMICS THE FORM OF THE BUILDING ENCLOSES THE SAUNA'S WOODPILE. **TOP LEFT:** THE GEOMETRY OF THE SAUNA'S PRISM ROOF AND SEMICIRCULAR SUPPORT IMPARTS A SURREAL QUALITY.

OPPOSITE TOP: THE GABLE ROOF IS A TRIANGULATED STRUCTURAL TUBE, ELIMINATING THE NEED FOR RAFTERS OR TRUSSES. **BOTTOM:** THE SAUNA ITSELF HAS AN INTIMATE QUALITY, WITH WINDOWS PROVIDING VIEWS OF THE LAKE AND WOODS. **TOP:** THE FURNITURE IN THE PORCH REFLECTS THE SAME RATIONALIST QUALITY OF THE SAUNA. **MIDDLE:** A STRAIGHT-RUN STAIR, FLANKED BY TWO DOORS, LEADS TO THE PORCH UNDER THE PRISMLIKE ROOF. **BOTTOM:** THE INTERIOR OF THE SAUNA CONTRASTS WOOD DOORS AND PARTITIONS AGAINST THE BRICK ENVELOPE.

SAMENESS AND DIFFERENCE

THE AMERICAN PSYCHOLOGISTS Ernest Skaggs and Edward Robinson identified what they called the "paradox of similarity." The more that things appear to be similar, the more we recognize differences among them and the more those differences attract our attention. While Skaggs and Robinson used that paradox to describe how we learn, it has profound implications for architecture as well.

We organize buildings much as we organize our lives, according to things that are alike and not alike, the same and different. The two dominant ways of doing so involve pairing elements, which often leads to symmetrical arrangements, or contrasting them, which often leads to asymmetry. Indeed, much of the history of architecture divides along those lines—classical symmetry versus modern asymmetry—and yet those two ways of organizing the world tend to remain mutually exclusive. They rarely account for the paradox of similarity, where sameness and difference occur at the same time, in the same place, among the same things.

That paradox suggests a third way of organizing the world: through repetition. The more like things we put together, the more we see their similarities and their differences simultaneously, and the more we embrace the paradox of similarity rather than vainly try to resolve it. Of all of David Salmela's work, no project explores this idea of repetition more fully than his Wild Rice Restaurant.

Located on a hill above Lake Superior, the restaurant consists of a main dining room that overlooks the lake, connected by glass-enclosed bridges to a U-shaped kitchen and service building. Outdoor dining decks and an entrance bridge and deck attach to the east and west ends of the building.

With that simple organization, the restaurant becomes an essay in repetition, revealing the complexity and subtlety of what happens when we group like things. The repetition occurs most prominently in the roofs of the building, evident when you first drive up to it on your way to the parking lot. Like an accordion, the restaurant's gabled roofs form parallel rows, all with the same pitch and metal cladding. At first glance, they all seem alike, but the more you study them as you walk down from the parking lot and over the wooden bridge to the entry deck, the more you see their differences. The ridge heights of the roofs ascend as the land falls away, the eaves intersect at different heights, and breaks occur both along and between some of the roofs.

The windows in the restaurant play a similar game. As you walk along the bridge toward the entry, the square windows start small, with an irregular pace; get larger and taller along the outdoor deck; and culminate in one large square window above the entry door, as if to say you have arrived. Likewise, the square windows along the lakeside are smaller and divided at the lobby, and larger and undivided in the dining area. Meanwhile, in the dining room's clerestory, tiny square windows seem to bounce around, as if to mock the logic of the repetitive openings below.

Inside the restaurant, the repetitions continue. The most obvious example is found in the dining room, where the tables and chairs are all alike, arranged in rows, set with identical place settings, and illuminated by repetitive rows of downlights and wall sconces. We have so accepted this format in restaurants that we often overlook the very point this building makes: because of that repetitiveness, we recognize the differences among the people dining there. Sameness within an environment can highlight our uniqueness as human beings.

As if to make that point even more emphatically, Salmela has placed the wine rack between the lobby and dining area, encased it in glass, and turned it into a tower, complete with rolling ladders for access to either side. The bottles are all similar in size and shape and color, and yet within that sameness we can relish the almost infinite differences among the wines they contain. Repetition serves to eliminate the less important in order to bring to light that which is more important, be it in what we eat, wear, or inhabit.

Paradoxically, repetition can also bring with it the element of surprise. Along the back of the dining room, a series of full-height square windows gives a view across an outdoor space between the two parts of the building to an identical series of windows in the service wing. Looking across that gap, you expect to see the same: people dining.

TOP: AN ELEVATED WALK LEADS TO THE ENTRANCE OF THE WILD RICE RESTAURANT FROM THE UPHILL PARKING LOT. **MIDDLE:** A SERIES OF PARALLEL GABLES INCREASES IN HEIGHT TOWARD THE ENTRY TO THE MAIN DINING ROOM. **BOTTOM:** A ROW OF LARGE SQUARE WINDOWS AND A SCATTERING OF CLERESTORY OPENINGS PROVIDE VIEWS OF THE LAKE.

But instead you look, unexpectedly, into the kitchen serving area, related to but different from the dining going on around you.

Another paradoxical aspect of repetition is that it often leads us to want repetition to come to an end. Evolution offers an example. While it involves the endless repetition of mutations, some of which improve the chances of survival, we like to find purpose in it, a culmination in something better. In architecture, that thinking leads to the notion of ideal form.

At Wild Rice, the main dining room plays the role of the ideal. Set apart from and seemingly evolved out of the "imperfect" gables of the service building, the symmetrical gabled form of the dining wing appears at first more "perfect" and complete. And yet, after setting us up to believe this, Salmela undercuts it. The dining wing, for instance, shares a white-walled light well with the service wing, underscoring the idea that, however "ideal" and autonomous the dining wing may be formally, it remains visually connected to and functionally dependent upon the kitchen.

The lesson here is that the paradox of similarity cuts both ways. Not only does the repetition of similar things emphasize the difference among them, but so too do the differences among things evolve out of the repetition of similar things. Such has been the case with wild rice, a grain that has evolved into a seemingly infinite number of varieties, all from the same type of grass. And such is the case with Wild Rice, one of the highest-rated restaurants in the Upper Midwest, whose similarities and differences serve us a visual feast.

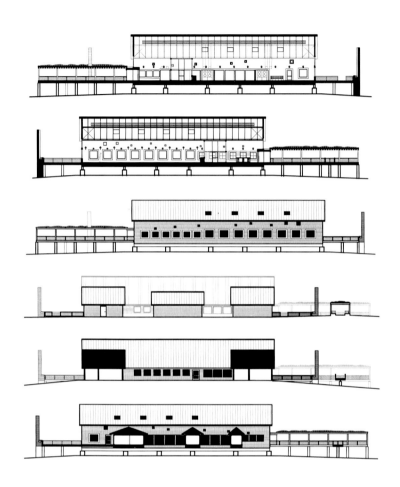

BELOW: A COVERED CANOPY EXTENDS FROM THE ENTRANCE, PROVIDING A VIEW OF LAKE SUPERIOR BELOW. **OPPOSITE:** A STORAGE BUILDING SHIELDS THE SERVICE COURT AND KITCHEN ENTRY FROM THE FRONT.

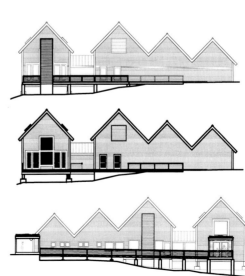

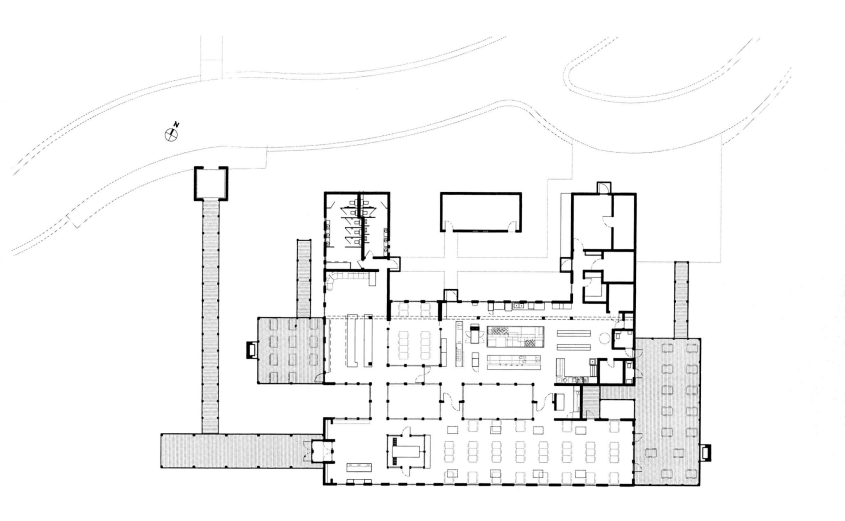

PAGES 30-31: THE LOBBY FEATURES A GLASS-ENCLOSED WINE RACK, WHOSE MULLIONS RECALL THE SQUARE WINDOWS OF THE DINING ROOM. **OPPOSITE:** THE TALL, GABLED INTERIOR SPARKLES AT NIGHT, WITH A LAYER OF LIGHTS SUSPENDED AMONG THE TRUSSES.

TRUE AND FALSE

TO UNDERSTAND what makes David Salmela's Albrecht house so compelling, look at its central grass court. Surrounded on three sides by the brick-clad, L-shaped house, the courtyard has a low bluestone wall around it, making the space visible but inaccessible to visitors, an "excluded middle." You can see it as a visual pun on Aristotle's "principle of the excluded middle": the idea that, as he said, "there is nothing between asserting and denying," that everything is either true or false and that nothing lies between. The Albrecht house offers a spatial equivalent, and a critique, of that idea. At every turn, Salmela presents you with a series of choices, none of which is obviously right or wrong, gaining your attention in the process.

The first such choice occurs the moment you approach the house. Two widely separated garages face the street, each with the same gabled roof, the same outward appearance. Which is the real garage? Salmela and his landscape architects, Jon Stumpf and Shane Coen, provide a hint with a paved drive up to one and a grass-strip drive to the other, but only after exploring a while do you find that the one serves as the main garage and the other as storage for an extra vehicle. When we seek the truth, different things sometimes look the same.

Up the paved drive, however, a third garage—this one with a flat roof—angles off from one of the gabled ones. Is one the real garage and the other something else? Salmela plays with the language he just established and reverses it: these two garages have the same function and a different look, as if to say that to find the truth, we also have to get past appearances.

The choices continue as you walk around the court, under a trellis, to two different front doors in the back wing of the house. The first door you come to is solid wood, painted white; the second is a pair of glass doors, set back slightly. Which is the "true" entrance? Does the solid door suggest privacy, a service entrance perhaps, or formality, the front door? Or do the recessed glass doors suggest openness as the main entrance or informality as the back door? In this case, it doesn't matter since both doors lead to a hall that runs the length of the house, connecting the main living and sleeping rooms.

All of those main spaces—kitchen, dining area, living room, and master bedroom—overlook the Mississippi River behind the house. In plan, the daytime and nighttime rooms interlock, with the prowlike solid of the master bathroom and closets sliding past the prowlike void of the living room, which culminates in a fireplace at its apex. Public/private, figure/ground, solid/void—Salmela plays his game of choice not only in elevation, but also in plan.

He does so in section too, using painted wooden slats of the same dimension for different functions. One set of slats divides the kitchen from the living and dining areas, enclosing the stair to the second-floor office, wrapping around the upstairs balcony, and turning into a rail for the stair that leads to a screened porch on the roof. The same-size slats also provide privacy over the large office window on the front of the house and some protection on the underside of the trellis around the court, in an intentional homage to Alvar Aalto's Villa Mairea.

The house also employs different forms for different purposes. A slate-clad box, enclosing the owner's second-floor office, sits on top of the brick-clad base of the main house. The living and working activities remain distinct, but by making the office visually dominant, with its tall, flat roof supported by an inverted steel-and-timber bowstring truss designed by engineer Bruno Franck, Salmela also raises questions as to the function of the house. Is it meant for living or as a base for working? In this age of the home/office, the answer may be either or both.

Truth can also be a fiction. The office, with its uncertain scale and large end window divided by crossed mullions, looks from the front of the house like a miniature church or public building. The adjacent screened porch and the campanilelike chimney reinforce this impression of the office having some public function. You find yourself wondering: What is a small-scale European village doing on the roof?

TOP: FROM THE STREET TWO DRIVES LEAD TO TWO GARAGES, WITH THE ALBRECHT HOUSE BEYOND. **MIDDLE:** THE GABLE-ROOFED GARAGE BOASTS A VARIETY OF BRICK, STONE, AND TILE CLADDING, LIKE A PRELUDE TO THE MAIN HOUSE. **BOTTOM:** THE STONE WALL AND TRELLIS LEAD TO THE BACK WING OF THE HOUSE, WHERE THE FRONT DOOR IS LOCATED.

Is it a comment on the dominance of work in our domestic lives or even on the public nature of the owner's business, as publisher of many local newspapers? Such fictions, however imagined, can suggest larger "truths" about us.

For all of its creative play around the idea of the excluded middle, the Albrecht house is anything but middling. Just the opposite. Challenging our assumptions, forcing us to make choices, asking us to look more closely—such are the things that this house shares with all great creative work. And that will always be true.

OPPOSITE TOP: A WOOD-SLAT CANOPY LEADS FROM THE DRIVE AROUND THE COURT, WHOSE GARDEN HOUSE SITS TO THE RIGHT. **MIDDLE:** THE COURT PROVIDES A PROTECTED PLACE FOR FAMILY ACTIVITIES AND OUTDOOR COOKING. **BOTTOM:** THE HOUSE STANDS ON A HIGH BLUFF OVERLOOKING THE MISSISSIPPI RIVER. **BELOW:** THE REAR ELEVATION SHOWS THE OFFICE AND SCREENED PORCH PERCHED ON THE BRICK BASE OF THE HOUSE.

OPPOSITE: A STAIR WITH A WHITE-SLAT RAILING SEPARATES THE DINING ROOM ON THE RIGHT FROM THE KITCHEN, LEFT. **TOP:** THE OFFICE, WHOSE STAIR LEADS UP TO A SCREENED PORCH, OFFERS A VIEW OF THE RIVER. **BOTTOM:** A STEEL-AND-TIMBER TRUSS SUPPORTS THE OFFICE ROOF AND CURVES OVER THE BALCONY.

ABOVE: RECYCLED TIMBERS FRAME THE CEILING OF THE LIVING ROOM, WHICH OPENS TO THE OFFICE ABOVE.
OPPOSITE: THE TALL, NARROW SCREENED PORCH FEELS LIKE A TREE HOUSE SITTING UP ABOVE THE RESIDENCE.

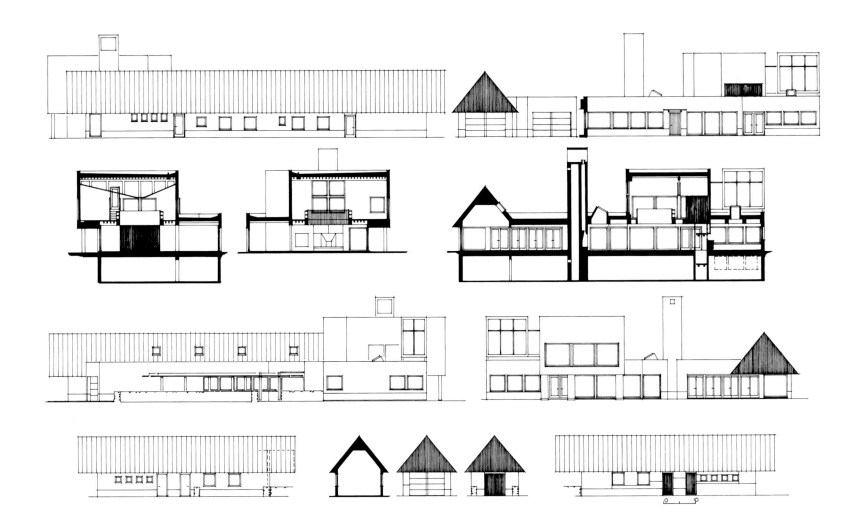

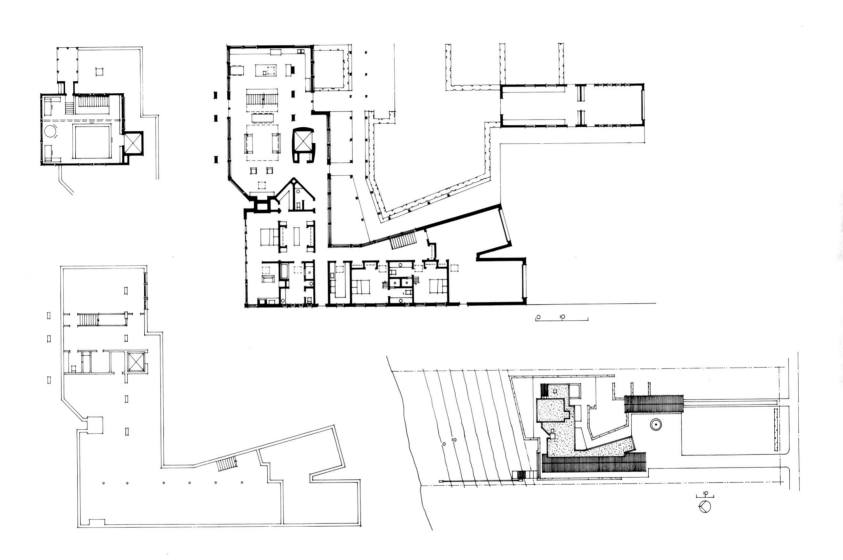

REALITY AND ILLUSION

PHOTOGRAPHY ENGAGES in illusion. It converts the three-dimensional world to a two-dimensional photographic surface, which viewers then reconvert into a three-dimensional mental image. The more powerful the photo, the more compelling the mental image and the more we are drawn into the illusion. Painting, of course, has historically done this as well, although much modern art has dismissed such illusionism, choosing empiricism instead, focusing our attention on the fact that we are looking at paint on a two-dimensional surface.

Architecture weaves a path between those two extremes, between illusionism and empiricism. It exists in three dimensions and yet comprises a series of two-dimensional planes; we construct its overall form and organization in our mind as we walk around it, and yet we also respond sensually to the patterns, textures, and colors of its surfaces. The power of architecture lies in that duality. It reminds us that the world is both real and imagined, both fact and interpretation, both flat and deep.

David Salmela plays off that idea in his design of the house and sauna for the photographer of his work, Peter Kerze. The house's façade appears to have a cube of horizontal siding sitting on top of and projecting from a vertical-sided base, which appears to recede from the face of the house. This is all an illusion, however. As you walk around the building, you quickly see that the upper wall of the house and its base occupy the same plane, with the only change occurring in the texture and color of the siding. The apparent projection of the upper part of the house occurs because the horizontally sided wall extends on one side, with a slight slope along the extension's bottom edge, while the apparent recession of the base derives from the continuation of the vertically sided wall at the other end, with a slight slope on its upper edge. As in a photograph, Salmela creates an impression of perspective on a two-dimensional surface.

The windows carry on this play of illusion against reality. A series of small square windows appears on both the upper portion and base of the house. Because the façade seems to exist in two different planes, the identical size of the square windows at once appears to contradict that illusion,

or to suggest that the lower windows are actually slightly larger than the upper ones, appearing to be the same size but farther away. Salmela groups three of the windows in a row and lets three others visually "float" in the wall, not lined up with each other or with any apparent floor levels within. This floating quality causes the windows to both project and recede visually, depending upon how you look at them. Meanwhile, the large translucent window cut out of the corner and stepping down along the side of the house looks at once as if it lies behind the façade and, because of its visual brightness, as if it projects from it.

The sauna (originally owned by Kerze's neighbor John Franks), completed twenty-one years after the 1979 house was built, employs a similar but subtly different game. A

small boxlike structure with a flat projecting roof, the sauna has vertical board siding, alternately stained red and left unstained. The red boards thus appear to pop forward, the unstained boards to step back, giving the flat wall a semblance of depth. The windows carry on the illusion, both visually and conceptually. A large four-square window adjoins the door, which looks narrow in comparison. On one side, a small square window, echoing those in the main

OPPOSITE TOP: THE FRONT OF THE HOUSE DISPLAYS A FLAT, FORCED PERSPECTIVE. **BOTTOM:** THE SCOTT-KERZE CABIN OVERLOOKS ST. MARY'S LAKE, WITH ITS SAUNA BY THE SHORE. **ABOVE:** INSIDE, THE EXPOSED STUDS AND PLYWOOD PROJECT A CABIN QUALITY.

house, floats high on the wall, while on the back and other side a horizontal strip window turns the corner and projects from both walls. One window looks too big, one too small; two appear to project beyond the wall, two literally do. Meanwhile, the sauna's fenestration suggests a kind of chronology—the modernist strip window, the rationalist square window, and the postmodernist four-square window—as if the building, constructed all at once, had evolved over time.

We have become accustomed to painting and photography fooling the eye, creating illusion or undermining our perception of reality. But architects have often played things fairly straight, much more enamored, especially in the modern era, with the idea of honesty or empirical truth.

Not so in the Kerze house and sauna. Salmela forces us, in these two simple buildings, to question the modernist claim of honesty and to ask where reality ends and illusion begins, even in something as tangible and three-dimensional as architecture. Also, since most of what we know about architecture comes from photographs of it, these structures beg the question, Where does the building end and the photograph begin in terms of our understanding? Can architects use the illusion possible in a photograph as a design tool? Can we learn from photography ways of giving depth to flatness? In this house for his photographer, Salmela makes illusion real and suggests that reality, at least at some level, remains an illusion.

TOP: THE VIBRANT SAUNA TAKES ITS PLACE AMONG OTHER NEARBY SAUNAS. **MIDDLE:** LIKE A BOAT DOCK PULLED ONTO SHORE, THE SAUNA'S DECK OFFERS A VIEW OF THE LAKE. **BOTTOM LEFT:** SLIDING WOOD PLATFORMS, BEAUTIFULLY CRAFTED, ALLOW PEOPLE USING THE SAUNA TO SIT OR RECLINE IN MANY DIFFERENT WAYS. **BOTTOM RIGHT:** THE SAUNA IS LIKE A COLOR PHOTOGRAPH IN CONTRAST TO THE HOUSE'S BLACK-AND-WHITE APPEARANCE.

AN UNCOMMON COMMONS

IN HIS 1968 ESSAY "The Tragedy of the Commons," biologist Garrett Hardin argues that whenever there exists space or resources available to all—what he calls the "commons"—individuals have an incentive to use it to their advantage, since they alone benefit from doing so, and a disincentive to maintain it for others, since everyone who uses the commons shares the cost of its exploitation. "Freedom in a commons," writes Hardin, "brings ruin to all." The political right has used Hardin's argument to propose selling off the commons, privatizing the public realm, while the political left has referred to his idea when calling for stronger government control of the commons, to protect the public realm. Both sides, however, have dealt with the tragedy by destroying the commons itself, either by eliminating it or fencing it off. And we see the results of such thinking all around us: suburban developments that carve most of the common land into private lots or gated communities that keep some land common but then keep most people out.

Jackson Meadow, a 145-acre residential development near the Twin Cities, offers an alternative, one worthy of emulation. Rather than divide the land into large lots as zoning allowed, David Salmela and landscape architects Shane Coen and Jon Stumpf clustered Jackson Meadow's sixty-four dwellings on only 30 percent of the land, creating a commons larger than the community itself. And rather than put up gates and fences to keep people out, they have designed five miles of trails that encircle the community and connect it to the St. Croix River and the town of Marine on St. Croix in the valley below.

When you drive up the wooded escarpment and across the undulating pasture that surrounds Jackson Meadow, you come upon a development that looks as if it had evolved over a long time. Most of the houses huddle in a tight grid, as in a traditional Scandinavian village, while a few others stand along what looks like a more recent suburban road that curves through the meadow. The town below served as the model for this two-part development. The designers adapted the grid pattern of Marine for their "village" lots and used the St. Croix River, lined with newer suburban houses, as the metaphor for the meandering road.

Other design decisions add to this sense of Jackson Meadow being out-of-time. The designation of the property as a planned-unit development allowed narrower rights-of-way, thirty-five feet versus sixty; narrower roads, eighteen feet versus twenty-four; and narrow open spaces, with no more than twenty-five feet between house and garage. And the designers' decision to face the village houses toward midblock pedestrian walks rather than toward the alleylike streets makes the place feel as if it predates the automobile. The only thing missing are the shops and other nonresidential buildings of a traditional town, giving Jackson Meadow away as a product of modern, single-use zoning.

The outlying houses also defy expectations. Varying in size and setback, they have relatively small areas of lawn, with tall meadow grass growing right up to their edges. Apart from the environmental benefits of leaving the meadow largely intact, this strategy blurs the boundaries between houses and emphasizes the shared responsibility this community has for the land.

That responsibility extends to the smallest details. The landscape architects, for instance, have placed utility lines under pedestrian paths to reduce rights-of-way, inverted the crowns of roads to channel storm water to catchment areas, and constructed wetlands in outlying areas to filter wastewater. Such innovations have demanded much public review, "but Marine also reevaluated and changed some of its codes because of it," Shane Coen says. The design tweaks cherished New Urbanist ideas as well, such as facing houses onto streets or thinking of open space as figural elements surrounded by buildings. Jackson Meadow inverts both, with the village's compact, pedestrian-oriented grid treated as a figure in nature. It's like the difference "between Seaside and Radburn," Coen says. "A Seaside-like design would have been overkill here. This is a rural place."

That reference to Radburn, with its mix of regionalism and modernism, applies to the architecture of Jackson Meadow as much as to its site plan. David Salmela considers himself a modernist, but he also believes that architecture must grow out of a region or tradition. "Modern buildings need to have a familiar quality to lure people in," he says, and that certainly applies to the houses here.

TOP: MUCH OF THE JACKSON MEADOW SITE PLAN BY COEN + STUMPF TREATS THE LAND AS AN ENVIRONMENTAL PRESERVE. **MIDDLE:** THE DEVELOPMENT LOOKS, AT FIRST, LIKE AN OLD VILLAGE OF METAL-ROOFED WHITE HOUSES. **BOTTOM:** THE HOUSES HAVE TRADITIONAL FORMS AND MATERIALS BUT MODERNIST PLANS AND MINIMALIST ELEVATIONS.

TOP LEFT: THE MILES OF TRAILS AT JACKSON MEADOW MEANDER THROUGH PRAIRIE AND WOODLANDS. **TOP RIGHT:** A NEW LINE OF SALMELA-DESIGNED HOUSES FORMS THE DEVELOPMENT'S OUTER EDGE. **BOTTOM:** GARAGES AND OUTBUILDINGS CREATE GATEWAYS AMD DEFINE OUTDOOR SPACES AROUND THE HOUSES.

Salmela has designed every structure in the place, using guidelines based on the scale and proportion of the nineteenth-century houses of Marine on St. Croix. "It's necessary to have rules in order to play within them," he says. "I'm not interested in stylistic rules, but I do believe in scale rules." In Jackson Meadow, no building exceeds twenty-four feet in width and all roofs must have a 12/12 pitch, for example. That, plus the uniform white color and common materials of wood cladding and metal roofs, all creates an ambiguity of influence. The white gabled buildings, with their punched windows and long, narrow proportions, give the place a historicist feel. Yet the repetitiveness of elements, the sparseness of details, and the continuity of forms along with the insistent whiteness bring to mind the housing developments of early modernism.

The same intertwining of tradition and modernism occurs within each house. Their compact shapes, symmetrical layouts, and light-filled interiors bring to mind the classic Nordic farmhouse, a vernacular that Salmela acknowledges admiring. But on closer examination, you realize that the main floor of most houses, with their objectlike cores and perimeter circulation, have a modernist free plan, with a continuous flow of space. That variability applies as well to the way each house extends out of doors. Most of the houses have detached garages that form tight, urbanlike spaces along one side, recalling the small yards of historic towns, yet most also have broad porches or terraces with ample doors and windows that blur the division between inside and out in a modern way. One house is almost all doors: twelve glass doors on the main floor, with none of them a "front" door.

The strength of Salmela's work lies in his ability to exaggerate the common, pushing the ordinary to a point where it seems strange and familiar at the same time. Some of this may come from his professed admiration of military facilities, full of "simple, beautiful structures, virtually the same, yet all different," he says. And it helps explain not just the architecture of Jackson Meadow, but also the nature of this community. Unlike most suburban developments, in which each house strives to emphasize the individuality of the owners, Jackson Meadow suppresses most such expression. While the houses themselves vary in plan and elevation, they are, like military facilities, virtually the same. "Why do we have this obsession with individual expression?" Salmela asks. "We have freedom, but why do we need to prove it again and again?" That echoes Garrett Hardin: "What does 'freedom' mean?" he asks. "Individuals locked into the logic of the commons are free only to bring on universal ruin; once they see the necessity of mutual coercion, they become free to pursue other goals. I believe it was Hegel who said, 'Freedom is the recognition of necessity.'"

Those who own houses in Jackson Meadow seem content with the mutual coercion they have embraced in both their houses and their land. Indeed, part of the appeal of the place lies in its difference from the values that drive most residential developments, which equate freedom with personal autonomy. Salmela argues that the pursuit of such freedom is futile. "In our drive for personal expression, we never get there," he argues. "In overstating our differences, we compromise our real diversity." Such thinking sets Salmela apart from most postmodernists, whose work his superficially resembles. It also sets him apart from many architects, who, after seeing Jackson Meadow, have commented that it looks "too institutional" or "too pure."

Such aesthetic judgments, though, miss the point of the place. While aesthetics play a major role in the self-identity of a community, what the place looks like may matter less than what the architecture and site planning provide in terms of social interaction and in terms of a "commons" people can care for. The whole may matter much more than its parts, which suggests that the tragedy of the commons may lie not in our individual exploitation of what we share with others, but in our looking at our social and environmental problems from the perspective of the individual. Other cultures, including that of the military, start from the perspective not of the individual, but of the group. And seeing development from the latter perspective is where Jackson Meadow's real contribution lies.

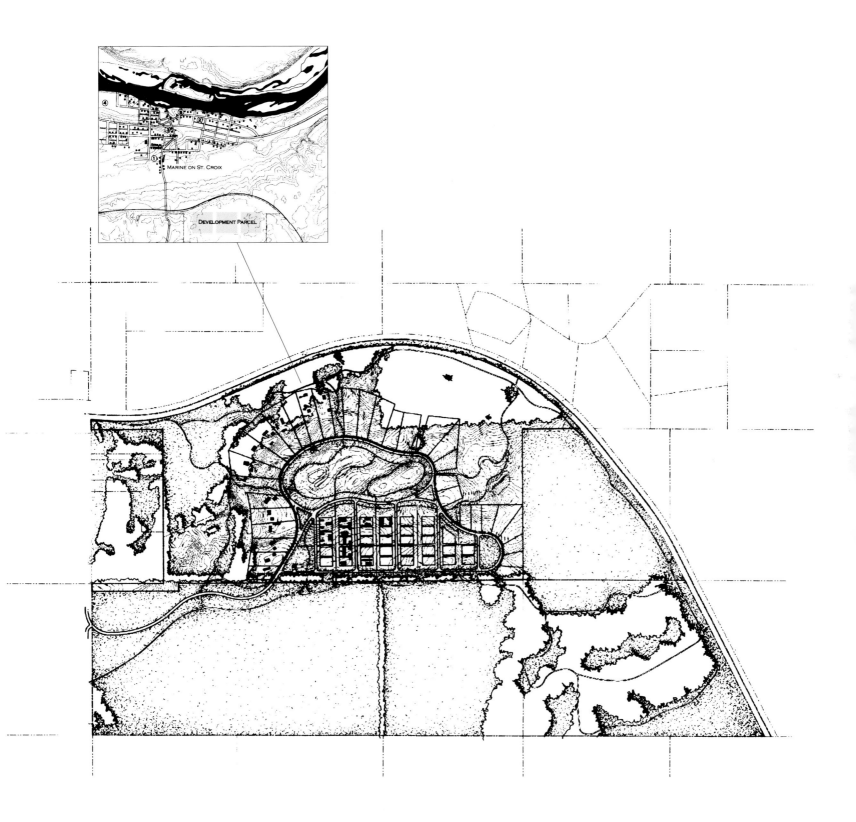

MARINE ON ST. CROIX

DEVELOPMENT PARCEL

TOP ROW: A ROW OF COLUMNS WITH EXAGGERATED CURVATURE, ROWS OF SQUARE WINDOWS AND FRENCH DOORS ALONG THE FACADE, AND A SLIGHTLY ASYMMETRICAL SIDE ELEVATION GIVE PERSONALITY TO THIS HOUSE AT THE CENTER OF THE COMMUNITY. **BOTTOM ROW:** DESIGNED FOR ARCHITECT CARL REMICK, THIS HOUSE AT THE EDGE OF THE DEVELOPMENT HAS A SYMMETRICAL FRONT AND REAR ELEVATION WITH ASYMMETRICALLY PLACED OUTBUILDINGS AND A DONALD-JUDD-LIKE PERGOLA LEADING TO THE SIDE ENTRY AND BACKYARD PRAIRIE.

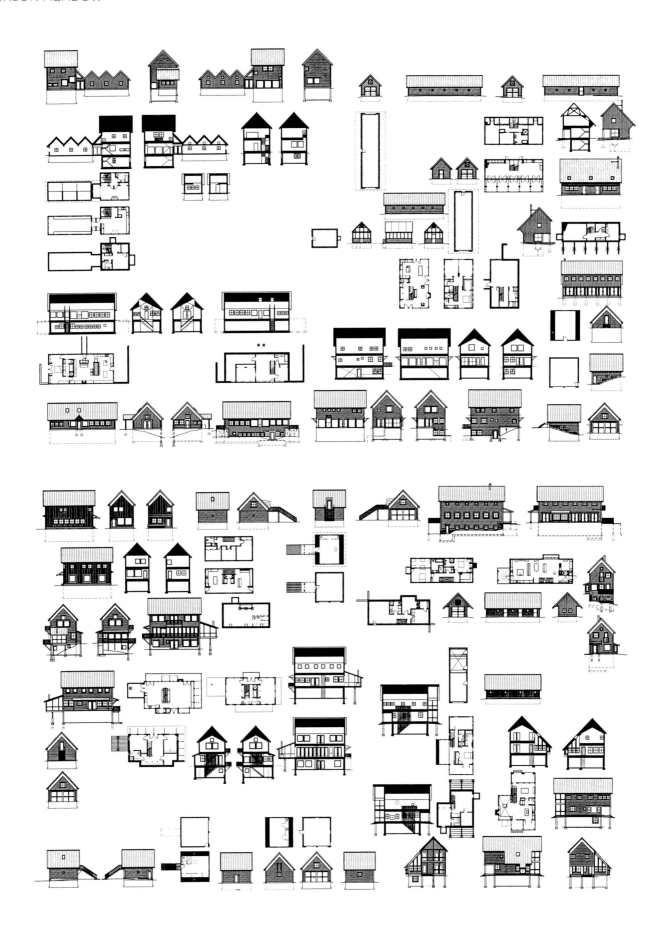

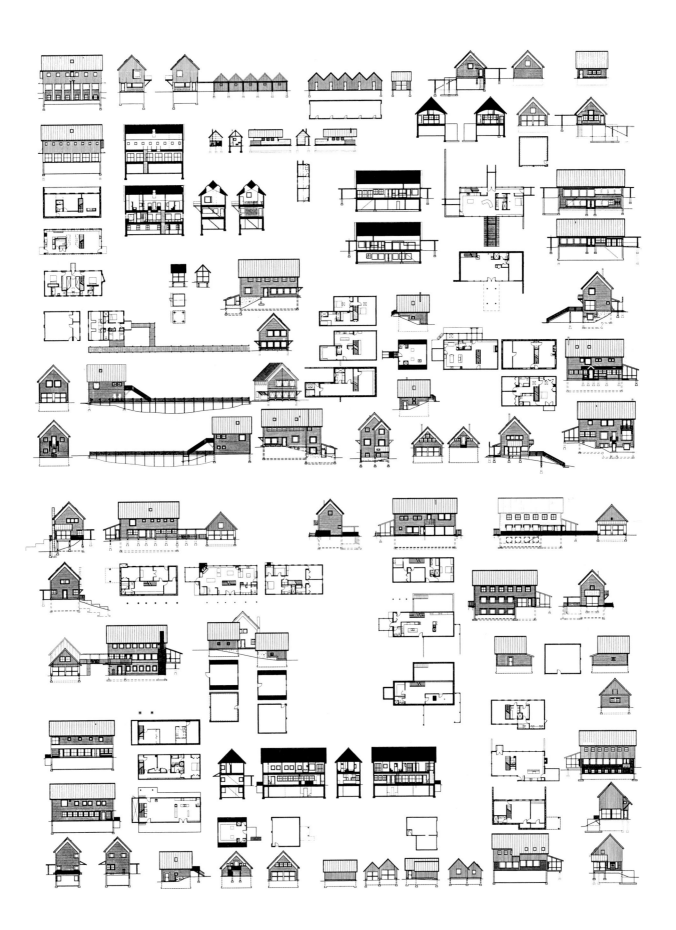

SPACE AND TIME

THINK ABOUT how we depict space and time. With space, we either draw lines around a space, indicating its dimensions or boundaries, or we draw points or objects within a space, suggesting its infinite expanse. The same occurs with time. We either draw lines or circles, representing the continuity or cycles of time, or we draw points or marks, denoting moments within the infinite expanse of time. Intellectual warfare has been waged over these differences. The distinction between modern and both pre- and postmodern architecture, for example, has often rested on the contrast between buildings that stand as objects in space versus buildings that define or enclose outdoor space, and on the contrast between buildings that mark the current moment in time versus buildings that refer to continuities over time.

But such polarities, while useful mental constructs, can distort reality. As David Salmela's Jones farmstead shows, architecture—like life itself—often exists at both poles at once. Look at how he has handled space in and around the house. When you first see it from afar, across the undulating fields of southern Minnesota, the Jones house appears as a tight cluster of metal-roofed buildings, marking a point in a seemingly infinite expanse of plowed fields and prairie. As you drive to it on its hill, it looks even more like an object in space. Its steep gable roofs, its long, windowless garage wall, its rounded end wall like some fortress keep, its towerlike chimney and cupola lookout—all convey a sense of this as a protected place, giving shelter against the open terrain.

But that changes as you come to a stop in the forecourt, a long, narrow space between the garage and the house. Here, all of a sudden, you feel as if you have entered an urban street, with doors and passageways and various-sized windows along it. Walking through the open passage between two parts of the house, you come upon a tree-shaded courtyard, enclosed on three sides by the house, with a concrete wall defining the fourth edge, a bulwark against the prairie that rises behind it. As in the traditional farmstead, with its farmyard embraced by a collection of buildings, the point in the distant landscape has become a

place that surrounds you. The object in space has become a space-defining object.

A somewhat different sense of space occurs inside the house. One wing contains the main living spaces, with a library, living room, dining room, breakfast room, and kitchen lined up under a long, wood-clad gabled ceiling. With full-height glass walls on either side, a view through the fireplace and china closet down the center of the room, and a white-painted mezzanine that seems to float on the timber beams overhead, this wing evokes the expansiveness of space, its linear and lateral extension off to the horizon. The other, parallel wing of the house does the opposite. Containing an office and guest quarters, this wing has a series of discreet rooms lit by a series of small- and medium-sized square windows, like those of a chicken coop. Overhead, slanted wood slats, as in a corncrib, line a mezzanine resting on timber post and beams. Here, the focus lies on the enclosure of space, on its boundaries and limits, with little concern with what lies beyond.

What the Jones farmstead does with space it also does with time. From afar, it looks starkly modern, a gleaming silver set of forms off in the distance. As you come closer, you see the house instead as an accumulation of different materials—metal roofs, granite-aggregate block walls, brick- and slate-clad walls, board-and-batten walls, log walls—that look as if they had accrued over a long time. Indeed, the house suggests a kind of fiction not uncommon in these parts: beginning as the one-room log house, expanding with the small-windowed guest wing, and eventually growing to include the glass-walled living wing, with a master-bedroom wing in between that itself had a shed roof lean-to that looks as if it were added at some point.

That mix of the modern and the modified occurs inside and around the house as well. The guest wing's living room may look ancient, with its massive log walls and huge timber beams, but walk outside and behind it and you will see that this "log house" cantilevers over an open storage area below, sitting on a concrete wall and columns like some archaic version of Villa Savoy. The office and bedrooms in the guest

TOP: LIKE A SHIP ON THE PRAIRIE, THE JONES FARMSTEAD APPEARS TO FLOAT ABOVE THE SWAYING GRASSES. **MIDDLE:** IN WINTER THE COURT, WITH ITS OUTDOOR FIREPLACE, PROVIDES SHELTER FROM THE WIND. **BOTTOM:** THE AUTO COURT OCCUPIES A NARROW, URBANLIKE SPACE BETWEEN THE GARAGE AND HOUSE.

wing offer a similar twist on time. Their many small windows suggest that these rooms have resulted from the renovation of an old barn or stable, and yet the simplicity of the interior details and the insertion of modern elements, such as the wood-slat rails and open-tread stairs, indicate the modernity of the wing. The living-room wing flips those relationships. Feeling initially like a modernist, glass-walled pavilion, with its floor-to-ceiling windows along most of its length, the wing's individual elements—such as the huge iron stove or the massive wood trusses along the mezzanine—look as if they were taken from older buildings (as indeed the trusses were) and installed in this new structure.

What difference do these differences make? While some architects continue to fight the battle between mod-

ernism and either pre- or postmodernism, David Salmela demonstrates in the Jones farmstead the futility of that warfare. The house shows how the polarized way in which we typically think about space and time represents not a difference of kind but of degree. What looks like an object in space from one perspective can be a space-defining object from another, and what seems like a product of its own time can also be an expression of change over time. And, in both cases, the opposite is also true. We can't debate issues of space and time, in other words, unless we define the scale or the speed of our observations. In this, as in so many other ways, the Jones farmstead puts us in our place.

LEFT: THE APPROACH REVEALS THE BLADELIKE CHIMNEY, THE SHIPLIKE STAIR, AND THE SILOLIKE END WALL. **ABOVE:** THE NARROW LIVING/DINING/KITCHEN WING ALLOWS VIEWS OF THE LANDSCAPE THROUGH WALLS OF GLASS. **BELOW:** THE SERVICE WING OF THE HOUSE INCLUDES A LOG STRUCTURE CANTILEVERED OVER AN EQUIPMENT STORAGE AREA.

THE TRADITIONAL STOVE SITS BETWEEN WOOD CABINETS AND BENEATH THE WHITE-PAINTED MEZZANINE.

A CENTRAL AXIS VISUALLY CONNECTS THE DINING ROOM, BREAKFAST ROOM, AND KITCHEN BEYOND.

ABOVE: A MEZZANINE CREATES A LOWER CEILING ABOVE THE LIVING ROOM AND ITS SEE-THROUGH FIREPLACE. **MIDDLE:** THE SEMICIRCULAR LIBRARY MAKES THE GABLE ROOF LOOK AS THOUGH IT CURVES TOO. **TOP RIGHT:** THE WOOD-LINED ENTRY DIVIDES LIVING SPACES FROM THE MASTER-BEDROOM SUITE. **BOTTOM:** A BEDROOM ON THE MEZZANINE CAPS THE GALLERY AND HOME OFFICE.

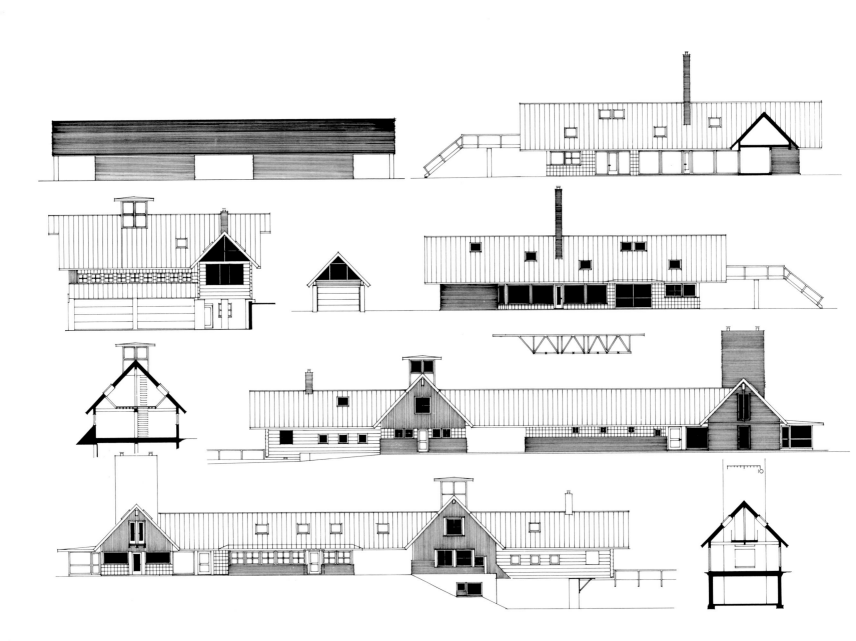

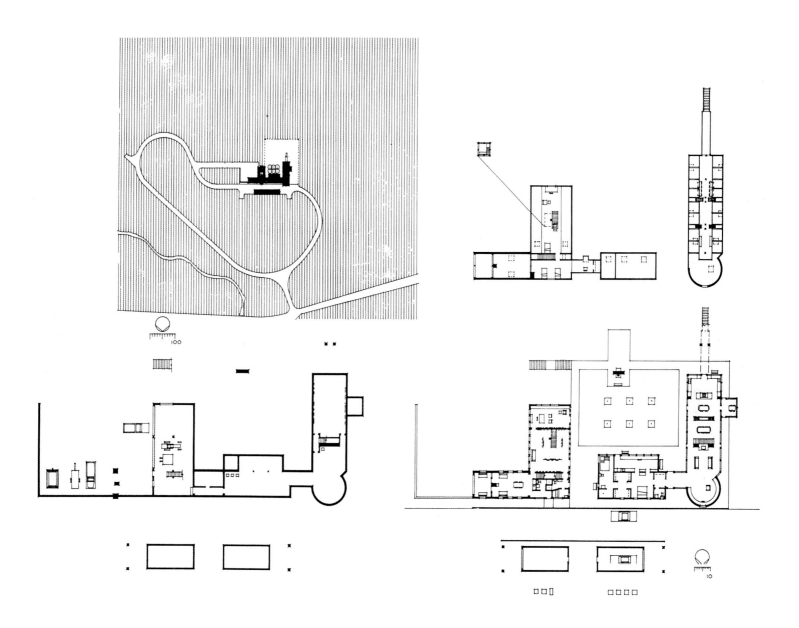

FRAMES AND FRAMING

WHAT DO WE DO when we frame? For all of the different uses of the word—be it framing the structure of a house or framing a piece of painter's canvas or framing a view through a window—its common meaning involves putting a boundary around something. We do this because of the unbounded nature of the world in which we live. The limitless horizons and seemingly endless complexity of our environment prompts us to frame some piece of it to understand and at least appear to control it.

But as soon as we do this framing, we tend to forget about it. We cover the frame of the building, turn the canvas around to paint, and attend to the view out the window rather than the window itself. It's as if, once bounded, we yearn to be free of the limits we have imposed upon ourselves. The retreat that David Salmela has designed for the Koehlers exemplifies this paradox.

Its largely glass-walled first floor, for instance, minimizes the window frames that might interfere with the hilltop view to Lake Superior and the forested landscape of Minnesota's north shore. At the same time, the regular rhythms of the windows, one after the other, provide an order that the world beyond seems to lack. The same is true of the plan of the main living spaces. Occupying one long room, the living, dining, and kitchen areas flow into each other, seemingly without boundaries. And yet that free plan has an order to it, provided by the stair, chimney, and storage unit that frame two vistas along both sides of the space. We want things framed without being framed by them.

The office and painting studio offer another take on this idea. The double-height studio juts out from one corner of the house, sheltered by an extension of the shallow gable roof. Two exterior columns hold up the end of the roof and visually frame the studio's glass wall, angled to the north. Here, the architecture expresses the idea of what occurs within. Art doesn't just frame a view of the world; it gives us a perspective on it, the artist's own skew. The angled geometry of this studio, with its forced perspective when viewed head-on, gives that idea a witty architectural expression.

The office offers yet another interpretation of the notion of a frame. A cluster of windows extends from desk height to the ceiling, with exterior trim wrapping the windows in the master bedroom above to create the impression from the outside of a single double-height space where none exists. It echoes the double-height windows of the studio on the opposite side of the house. But that single composition of office and bedroom windows also expresses the continuity of working and resting that constitutes life in the home office. Meaning arises from what we include in and exclude from a frame.

It also arises from projecting ourselves into what is framed. Take the wood-framed decks that extend from three sides of the structure: they create a kind of artificial ground plane hovering above the steeply sloped site, providing vertiginous views of the surrounding landscape. The decks also bring to mind those of a ship floating above the green sea of trees and making the long, narrow house seem like some ark, stranded on its mountaintop far above the receding waters.

That nautical feel continues inside the retreat, where the freestanding stair to the second floor has the character of a wooden gangplank with slatted sides, touching down on a platform accessible from both the living room and entry hall. Upstairs, the bedrooms, like the cabins of a ship, line a single-loaded corridor, with each room having a slightly projecting window, like large, square portholes.

ABOVE: THE KOEHLER RETREAT PERCHES HIGH ABOVE THE VALLEY WHEN VIEWED FROM THE SOUTHEAST. **OPPOSITE TOP:** THE ENTRY FROM THE NORTH OPENS TO A DRAMATIC VIEW OF LAKE SUPERIOR. **BOTTOM:** THE SOUTH DECK ALSO PROVIDES A COMMANDING VIEW, WITH WINDOWS THAT PROJECT TOWARD IT.

The projection of the windows on the second floor also makes them seem to telescope toward the view, like a camera's zoom lens. We have become so accustomed to seeing the world from within a photographic frame that it now seems normal, to the point where reality mimics its representation through film. The windows here offer an example. They seem to frame the view from each room deliberately, like still photographs. On the corridor side, the bank of windows provides a series of views as you walk down the hall, like frames of videotape. Life becomes like our movies of it.

The idea of framing culminates in the belvedere on the roof, a miniature of the building below. With glass on all sides, the belvedere has no function other than to provide, as its name indicates, a beautiful view. And, like the entire retreat, the belvedere suggests that we frame houses not just to provide shelter or to put up boundaries, but to provide a vantage point from which we see the world. "Look at this!" the Koehler retreat seems to say. And look we will.

OPPOSITE: THE ENTRY OPENS PAST THE STAIR TO THE MAIN LIVING AREA OF THE RETREAT. **BELOW:** THE KITCHEN AND DINING AREA ALSO OCCUPY A PART OF THE MAIN LIVING SPACE.

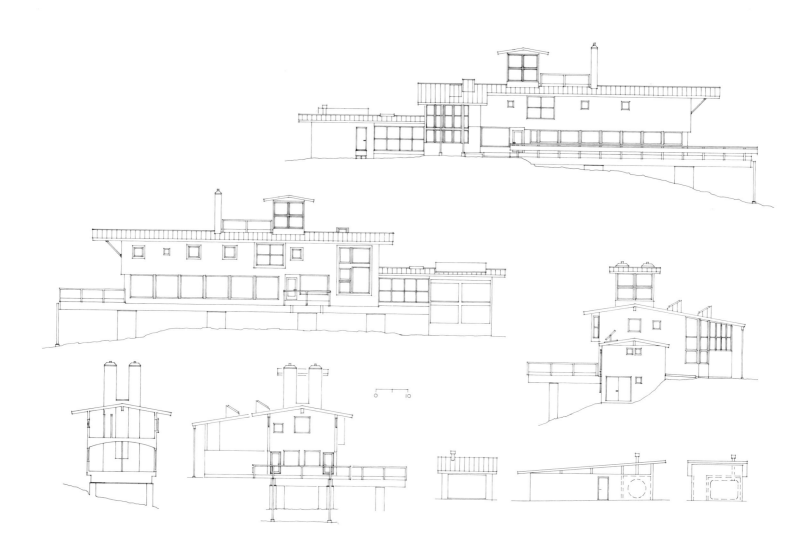

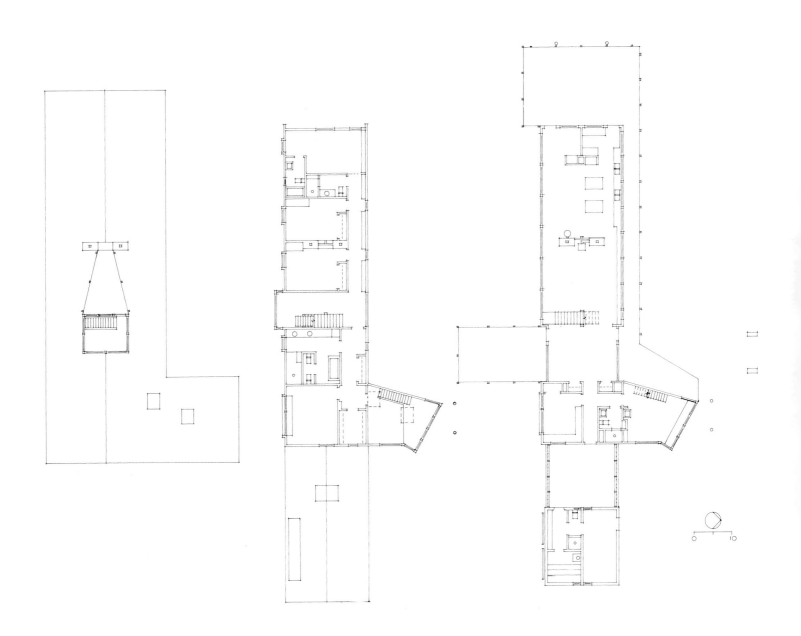

THE ELEMENTS OF NATURE

WESTERN THOUGHT BEGAN in the contemplation of nature, with the "pre-Socratic" philosophers defining reality in terms of the four elements: earth, air, fire, and water. While we rarely think of the world in this way anymore, we remain affected by these four elements and architecture still serves to protect us from or connect us to them.

David Salmela's Gooseberry Falls State Park Visitors Center shows how seriously architecture can take that role. Consider the building's relation to the earth. Its broad gable roof comes nearly to the ground along its back side, shielding the building from the nearby road while giving it the low-hanging forms of the surrounding conifers. Along the building's front, a series of timber columns marks a colonnade that leads you to the main hall, recalling the tree lines through the adjacent forest. These columns stand off the ground, bolted to steel plinths as if the earth had risen to meet the building or the ground around it had eroded. The sense of the earth continues inside, where black terrazzo floors connect to the bluestone paving outside and remind us of the black soil below, the product of centuries of fallen leaves and decaying trees.

While the visitors center brings you down to earth, it also gives you air. As you approach the entry along the colonnade, you see right through the main hall, with glass walls on either side of the space. It's like glimpsing a clearing through a stand of trees, finding air where you least expect it. Inside, the building has a cavelike quality. The service wing, with its exhibit space, theater, and gift shop, provides a dark back side, which makes the continuous glass walls opening to the east seem even brighter and airier. It's when we least expect them, though, that we see the elements anew. The main hall has a timber-framed gabled roof with a long steel beam that supports a triangular truss, all of which allow light to come in where it almost never does: at the roof ridge. That sky-lit ridge produces a surprising airiness, helping us feel the outdoors at the center of the room.

The element of fire has one prominent place in the building: the massive stone fireplace at the corner of the main hall. Recalling the stonework in the 1930s-era buildings elsewhere in the park, the fireplace consists of local boulders, laid in a random pattern and forming a tall chimney that merges into a stone wall wrapping the corner of the space. At the center of this mass of ashlar burns a fire. You find yourself drawn to the hearth not only because of the warmth it radiates, but also because of the potential destructiveness of the fire it contains. Fire, as the pre-Socratics knew, can destroy the products of the earth and consume the air.

And fire could be consumed only by water, an element that, at the visitors center, finds its place in the landscape. You hear the water in the thunderous sound of Gooseberry Falls that grows louder as you move from the parking lot along a path at the top of a ravine, through the building, and on to the massive cascade of water. And you sense the water's path as it sheds from the gabled roofs of the building, across the clearing beside it, and down to the river and lake. If architecture keeps fire contained, it sheds water, an equally destructive force in a building.

One of the ironies of our not thinking much about the four elements anymore is that we have come to abuse them: polluting the water and air, contaminating the earth, and burning too much fossil fuel. And buildings contribute to this abuse as sources of pollution, contamination, and combustion. This visitors center, with its landscape designed by Coen + Stumpf, suggests another course. The center minimizes impervious surfaces to let the earth absorb and filter the water that falls from the cedar-shake roof. It minimizes its alteration of the land and forest to let the foliage clean the air and protect the soil. And it minimizes the use of fossil fuel in vehicles, which remain parked near the entrance to the grounds, and inside the building, which partly heats the main hall with a wood-burning fireplace.

All of that accords with the larger purpose of the park: to educate the public about the natural environment. But the building furthers that message, showing how we can inhabit our surroundings in ways that enhance the world we still depend on for our survival. You come away from the visitors center more aware that in architecture, as in ecology, some of our most pressing concerns remain the oldest in western thought: earth, air, fire, and water.

TOP: THE GOOSEBERRY FALLS STATE PARK VISITORS CENTER SITS LOW ON ITS SITE BETWEEN THE PARKING LOT AND THE FALLS.
BOTTOM: A GLASS-WALLED CORRIDOR GIVES ACCESS TO A GALLERY AND A GIFT SHOP BEYOND.

ABOVE: THE GREAT ROOM CULMINATES IN A STONE FIREPLACE THAT RECALLS NEARBY WPA BUILDINGS OF THE 1930S.

OPPOSITE: A GREAT STEEL TRUSS ALLOWS THE RIDGE OF THE ROOM TO BE GLAZED, LETTING IN NEEDED LIGHT.

A COLONNADE OF HEAVY TIMBERS UNDER A LOW ROOF LEADS TO THE MAIN ENTRY.

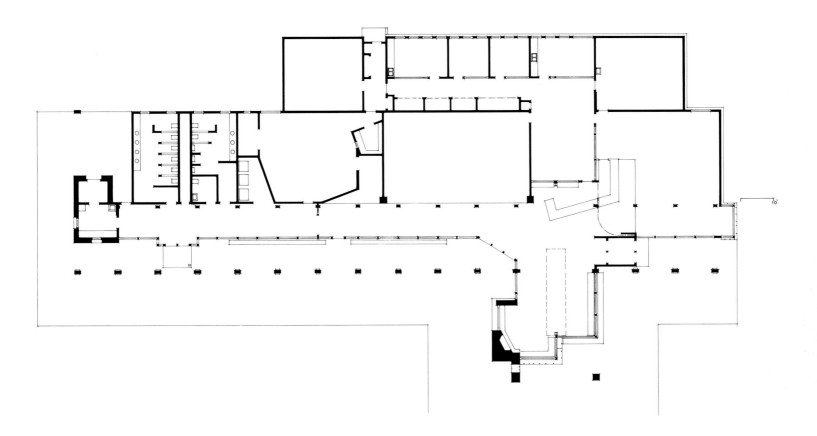

WHOLES AND PARTS

MODERN WESTERN CULTURE often traps us between what the philosopher Ken Wilber calls the "ego" and the "eco," between those who seek meaning through the expression of the self and those who seek it through the elevation of nature. Both loom large in the architectural culture, with egotistical design superstars on one side and rabid environmental activists on the other. And yet, as Wilber observes, both positions mistakenly posit one entity—the self or nature—as a whole to which all other things must bend.

To escape this trap, Wilber argues, we must see everything, including ourselves, as wholes and as parts of larger wholes at the same time. In architecture, that idea lies, often unrecognized, in the vernacular. Such work rarely interests either the "ego" or "eco" crowd, since one side finds vernacular buildings insufficiently self-expressive and the other, insufficiently obedient to nature. Even those who embrace vernacular architecture often misunderstand it, seeing it as an escape from rather than an engagement with the problems of the world.

David Salmela's Smith residence, one of the most overtly vernacular houses he has designed, suggests a new way of understanding the role such architecture can play. The clients requested that the residence look as much like a traditional Finnish farmhouse as possible, and Salmela has met their wishes. But in doing so, he gives them something that looks not to the past but forward, transcending the ego/eco, self/nature polarity that so plagues us.

Like a Finnish farmstead, the Smith house consists of a red-painted outbuilding and an ochre-colored house. The multigabled outbuilding consists of two garages that form a wall between the parking area and the house, framing an entry path that leads to the front door. The house itself comprises a two-story gabled rectangle, with one-story vestibule wings projecting from either side. Tall transom windows illuminate the high-ceilinged living spaces that flow one into the other on the first floor. The small second-floor windows light three bedrooms, two bathrooms, and a double-height space over the entry and dining area.

The house has a superficial resemblance to a Finnish homestead, with its tall first floor and high attic, its classical proportions and casual asymmetry, and its mix of board-and-batten and lap siding. But such appearances belie the real feat of this house: interpreting a modern residence with a mind-set that sees everything as simultaneously a whole and a part. In the garage structure, Salmela starts with the parts—six individual gabled bays—and lines them up, side by side, to form a larger whole that meets several needs—enclosure, security, entry, privacy—all at once. Meanwhile, in the house, he starts with the whole—a simple, gabled form—and articulates its parts in ways that reinforce the entire composition. The transom windows, for instance, repeat the proportions of the entire building, with regulating lines that determine the location of such things as the second-floor sill or the projecting vestibule.

We often see such order as "classical" and thus irrelevant to the "modern" world. But, as Ken Wilber points out, our ability to sustain ourselves as a species depends upon our understanding an order in which we must balance our rights as individuals—as parts—with our responsibility to the whole. This is not some out-of-date "classical" notion, but an idea of relevance to the most pressing environmental, social, and political problems we now face.

Look at what the Smith residence tells us about this. The house and outbuilding each sits as a whole, distinct from the land and relatively free of landscaping, and yet each also acknowledges the site as part of a larger ecosystem and so minimizes its impact on the property, leaving most of the land unaltered. Likewise, the house and outbuilding remain wholes unto themselves, separate from each other and opposite in color and expression. At the same time, the two create a larger whole, in a composition with the adjoining tree, which forms a defined social space needed in this landscape of empty horizons.

Parts and whole continue inside the house. The main floor consists of essentially a single room, a whole that encompasses several parts: living area, dining space and kitchen, toilet room, fireplace, and stair. Yet that whole is a part of the land and sky around it, brought in through the high windows that repeat around the room. At the same time, the whole of each of the three bedrooms upstairs becomes

TOP: THE BRIGHT COLORS AND SIMPLE FORMS OF THE SMITH RESIDENCE COMPLEMENT THE BROAD, OPEN SITE. **MIDDLE:** THE MULTIPLE GABLES OF THE GARAGES ECHO THE ELEMENTAL QUALITIES OF THE HOUSE. **BOTTOM:** THE SPLIT GARAGES FORM A GATEWAY TO THE ENTRY COURT, OFFERING A SENSE OF PROTECTION.

a part of a larger whole of the house, with a walkway that looks down to the dining area and entry and that looks out in a rhythm of windows determined by that of the overall order of the façades.

While such architectural moves may seem only symbolic, they serve to constantly remind us of our simultaneous autonomy and connectedness. And at a time when the modern world seems terribly confused about such things—thinking that bigness equals wholeness and parts mean fragmentation—we need such reminders about our place in the world, reminders such as those the Smith house provides.

LEFT: A TWO-STORY SPACE DEFINES THE CROSS-AXIAL ENTRY AND DINING AREA. **BELOW:** THE MAIN LEVEL IS ESSENTIALLY ONE LARGE ROOM DIVIDED BY A FIREPLACE. **OPPOSITE:** THE OCHRE BOARD-AND-BATTEN EXTERIOR OF THE HOUSE CONTRASTS WITH THE RED GARAGES.

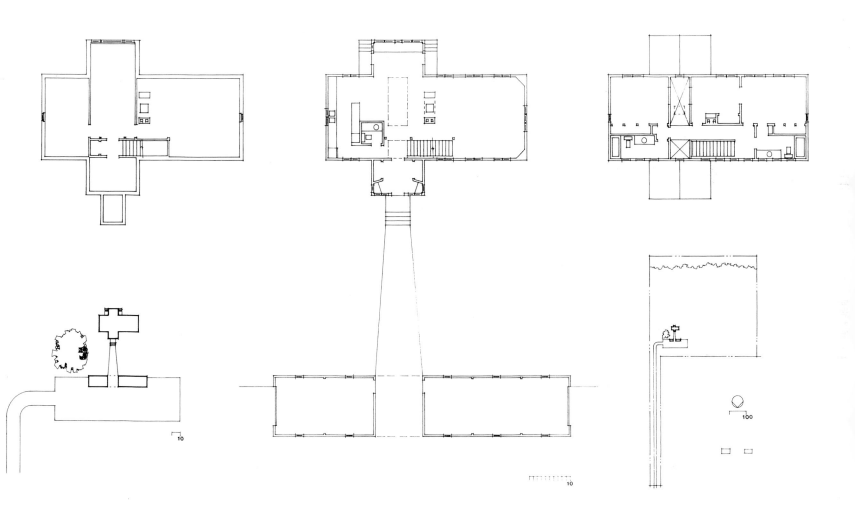

BODIES AND BUILDINGS

MODERN ARCHITECTURE, like modern medicine, has long seen buildings and bodies in the same way, as sets of systems: structural systems, circulation systems, cooling systems, waste systems, and so on. David Salmela's Loken house draws a different parallel between bodies and buildings, one that is both premodern and resonant with our postmodern times. The Loken house presents the building and the body not as a machine made up of systems, but as ecologies, inseparable from their context and indivisible into mind, body, and soul. It emphasizes the importance of wholes as much as parts, environments as much as systems.

Consisting of an existing residence that has been altered and added to, the Loken house shows how much a holistic view of health involves not wholesale replacement, but the grafting of new onto old. Salmela's renovations of the existing house fit seamlessly into the colonial revival original, from the glass-enclosed entrance inside a former front porch to the living room's asymmetrical wood-fireplace surround in an exaggerated colonial profile, to the wood-cabinet kitchen with its brightly colored breakfast nook under a bent-plywood ceiling. These new elements transform the existing spaces and make you realize that, in architecture as in life, it's a matter of doing the best with the body you've got.

It's also a matter of doing something for the mind and soul at the same time. A Ping-Pong room, with a loft overhead, constitutes one of the major additions to the Loken house: a space for recreation, with nooks in which to retreat and balconies from which to contemplate the world below. The shaped ladder-stair to the loft embodies the soulful quality of that room, looking as if it were designed for banister sliding.

For the mind, Salmela has designed a study and library tower on the south side of the house, perched on a concrete foundation above a steep slope. Connected to the first-floor deck and by an arched bridge to the second-floor master bedroom, the tower offers a view inward as well as out, with varied windows—some clear and some divided, some broad and some narrow—that reflect the diverse directions of a mind at work.

Equally appealing to senses and spirit is the sauna, set north of the house among trees. Containing a tub room and sauna, the structure has a steep gable roof that comes down low over the outwardly battered clapboard walls, like some ancient mountain shelter intended to shed snow. Its windows, with mullions in the form of a pinwheel, let light into the narrow building and hint, with the four directions of the divided lights, at the actions that occur within: sitting, standing, lying down, and submerging.

Also expressive of what occurs within is the three-car garage, relocated from a site at the edge of the embankment. The garage has three parallel gable roofs, with inwardly tapered doors on one side and small square windows on the other. Rarely do utilitarian buildings respond to their contents as this one does, with roofs like the cars within, tapered doors echoing the bottom-heavy section of autos, and small windows, two per bay, reflecting the headlights of each vehicle.

Salmela takes the idea of the building expressing the body within to an even greater height in the stable, built after the rest of the house's renovation and additions. Like the head and neck of the horses corralled within, the stable's profile has a haunch-gable roof, whose trusses follow the rise and fall of the exterior walls. The projecting end gable, terminating in a carved ridge beam, furthers the equine analogy, as if the stable were leaning forward to a trough. The irregular heights of the windows, the brightly colored cladding, and the openings at front and back all continue the metaphor of the house in the guise of a horse.

We have become unaccustomed to such anthropomorphic architecture because we have become unused to seeing buildings and bodies as much more than accumulations of systems and assemblies of parts. As a result, we often miss the fact that both buildings and bodies quite literally "house" us, something that premodern societies understood well. The Loken house recalls that tradition without becoming too literal or returning to the machine metaphor that remains a kind of bad habit of architects, and doctors too. Instead, the various parts of the house retain a sense of wholeness, both within themselves and in relation to each other. And in them, we in turn see ourselves.

TOP: THE STABLE'S JUMPING ELEVATIONS AND HUNCHED FORM BRING TO MIND THE BODY OF A HORSE. **BOTTOM LEFT:** IN THE KITCHEN, A BRIGHTLY COLORED BREAKFAST ALCOVE FEATURES A BENT-PLYWOOD CEILING. **BOTTOM RIGHT:** A WOOD STAIR, EQUALLY MODERN AND VERNACULAR, CONNECTS THE PING-PONG ROOM TO A LOFT.

TOP LEFT: THE MANTEL, CONCEALING AN EXISTING FIREPLACE, SHOWS THE SLIGHT ASYMMETRIES OF CRAFT PIECES. **TOP RIGHT:** THE SAUNA, WITH ITS STEEP ROOF AND LOW EAVES, RECALLS THE SHEDLIKE SAUNAS IN SCANDINAVIA. **BOTTOM LEFT:** THE LADDER-STAIR, WITH ITS SHAPED SIDEBOARDS, ENHANCES THE FEELING OF CHILDHOOD FANTASY. **BOTTOM RIGHT:** THE SLANTED BOARD WALLS GIVE PROTECTION AND PRIVACY WHILE PROVIDING LIGHT TO BOTH FLOORS.

SNOW HIGHLIGHTS THE LOKEN COMPOUND'S BRIGHT COLORS AND VARIED ROOF ANGLES.

THE LIBRARY AND STUDY TOWER PROJECTS OVER THE SLOPE AND TOWARD A VIEW OF LAKE SUPERIOR.

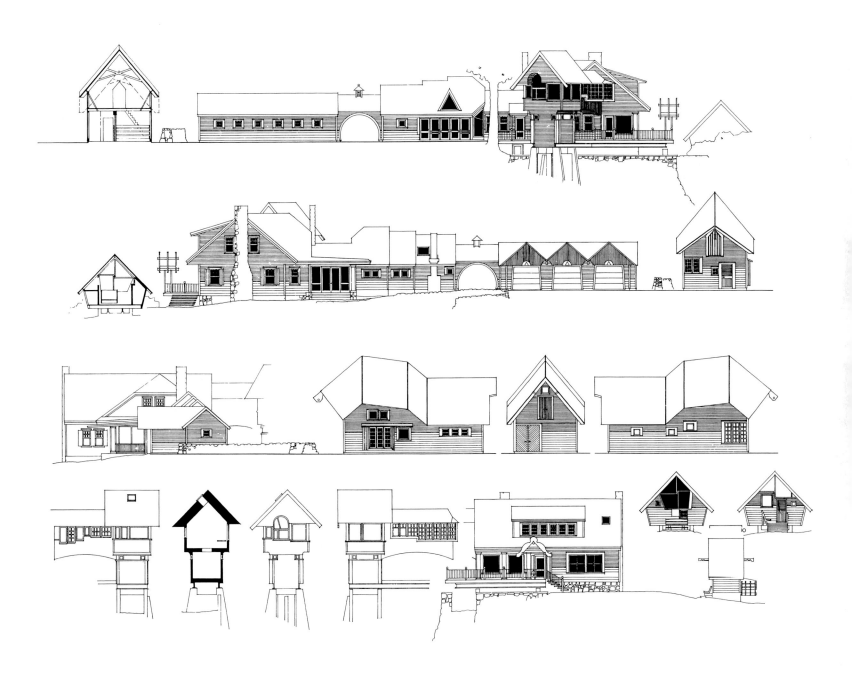

HUMANS AND NATURE

THE CHALLENGE OF LIVING involves two types of relationships: our relationship to the natural world and our relationship to the human world, to ourselves and other people. In providing the enclosures within which we live, architects have to deal with those two relationships, something recently done rather badly. Instead of relating people to the natural world, architects—led by engineers—have increasingly designed buildings that seal individuals off from the outside. And instead of relating people to each other, architects—led by lawyers—have increasingly designed buildings that keep individuals apart, each on his or her own property, and each within his or her own private space.

As a result architects have, ironically, eliminated much of the profession's reason for being by negating the relationships we have historically made through buildings. So when we encounter a building such as Salmela's Hanson retreat, which embraces these relationships and gives expression to their internal contradictions, it deserves our attention.

The retreat stands next to a large rock outcropping in a heavily wooded area of northern Minnesota overlooking a lake. The relationship it strikes with its dramatic natural setting is one of minimal intrusion. The main part of the narrow, rectangular structure runs parallel to the contours between the rock and a steep slope, and it stands mostly on concrete piles—design strategies aimed at minimizing its effect on the land. At the same time, the entry to the building, along a boardwalk and up a flight of exterior stairs adjacent to the rock face, makes you aware of its rugged terrain, while an outdoor covered bench, with an undulating back edge, echoes the rocky landscape and provides a place to look back over the terrain.

The form of the retreat also echoes its location. The roof, which rises and falls along the length of the structure, is a great curve that follows the upward slope of the rock outcropping and the downward slope of the site. The ancillary roofs of the office and storage shed, which project from the main building, also follow this slope, as if the retreat arose out of the ground in some tectonic upsurge, carrying the contours of the land with it.

The structure proposes a different relationship to nature than that which is common today. Rather than sit upon the land, alter its configuration, contrast with its form, and separate us from the local climatic conditions, the retreat wraps and steps over the land, provides places to sit in the sun or out of the wind, and opens itself to the view and the breeze. It is a modern building, but it embraces an ancient idea of architecture as a mediator between ourselves and nature, and as a preserver of the land upon which we depend.

The retreat does much the same as it relates people to each other. The modern idea of social relationships often pits the individualistic, antisocial rebel against the corporate, socially conservative traditionalist. While those two extremes sometimes join forces, such as the corporate sponsorship of the works of rebel artists, these types remain distinct and otherwise unrelated. An older tradition is one of cooperative relationships of individuals in small groups, a communalism in which the group acknowledges individual differences and yet expects them to work toward the good of the whole.

That finds an architectural expression here. The plan of the retreat has a large living/dining/kitchen room, with a service core separating it from the master bedroom and adjoining office. Up the stairs, or rather up a ladder, you find

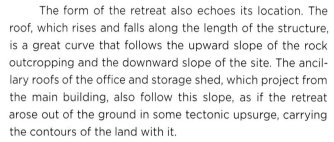

ABOVE: FROM THE DOWNHILL SIDE, THE HOUSE OFFERS MANY PLACES FROM WHICH TO ENJOY THE VIEW. **OPPOSITE TOP:** THE HANSON RETREAT'S ELEVATIONS SUGGEST INDIVIDUAL DIFFERENCES UNDER A COMMON ROOF. **BOTTOM:** A LARGE BOULDER DEFINES THE ENTRY PATH AND ANCHORS THE HOUSE ON ITS SLOPED SITE.

bunk rooms: tiny spaces that sleep two to four people in stacked, overlapping beds. A screened porch on both levels provides a mosquito-free view of the lake. The building, in other words, mixes spaces for individuals to be alone, together, or in various combinations, all under a great, arching roof that reminds you, wherever you are in the structure, of your place in relation to the group.

That idea finds similar expression in the retreat's elevations. Windows of various sizes and shapes—large and small, rectangular and square—jostle for space on the wall, some illuminating the big common room, others bringing light to a particular bunk. Inside, tiny openings in the wall above the living room give those in individual bunks a view of the common area. These various windows all have a functional rationale, belying their seemingly irrational pattern, but even more important is their symbolic role. The openings, in their own rough-and-tumble way, all reinforce the rise and fall of the curved roof, expressing through architecture the communal idea of individuals each contributing to the overarching good.

The Hanson retreat does more than stake out, in modern form, the old idea of architecture, helping us relate to the natural and human world. The structure also shows what architecture can contribute to our understanding of those relationships. In looking to technology to mediate between us and nature or the law to legislate our rights and obligations to each other, we have tended to seek broad, universal answers to those age-old problems, resulting in an increasingly automated and homogenous physical world. This building suggests that through architecture, we might instead seek smaller-scale and more site-specific answers to the challenge of living, for which the world, both natural and human, will be better off.

ABOVE: INSIDE, THE BUNKS (EACH WITH PEEPHOLES) OCCUPY THE LOFT ABOVE THE LIVING AREA. **RIGHT:** THE SCREENED PORCH PROVIDES NOT ONLY A PROTECTED OUTDOOR SPACE BUT ALSO A VIEW BACK TO THE HOUSE. **OPPOSITE:** THE BENCH AND ITS WING WALL FORM A PROTECTED PLACE IN AN EXPANSIVE LANDSCAPE.

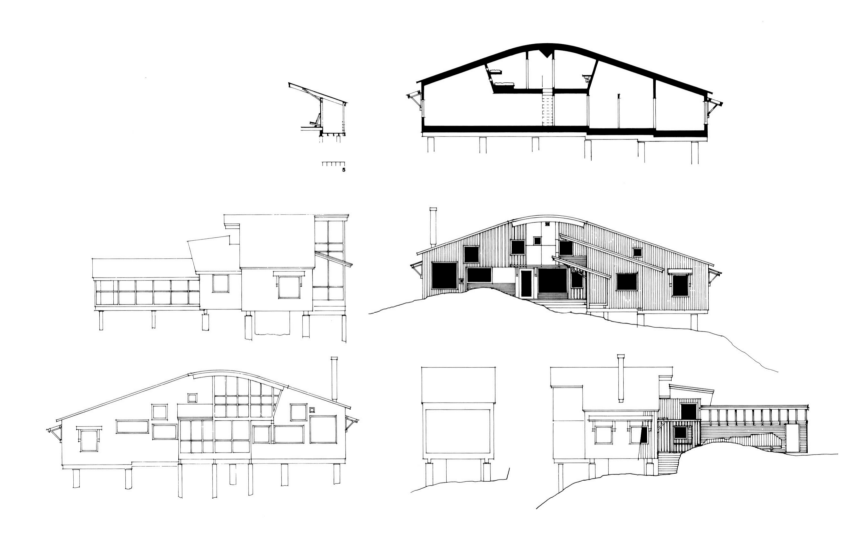

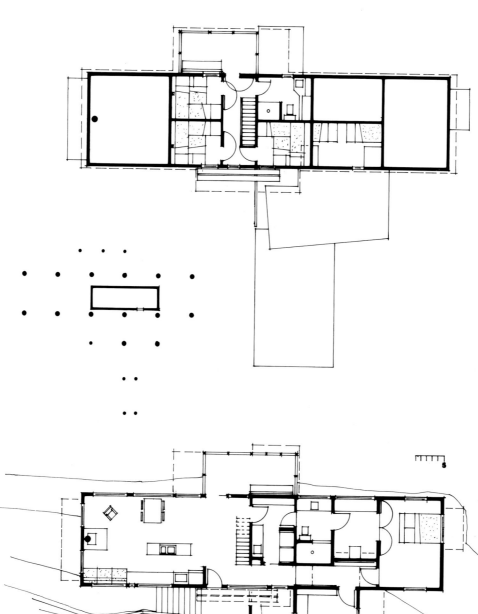

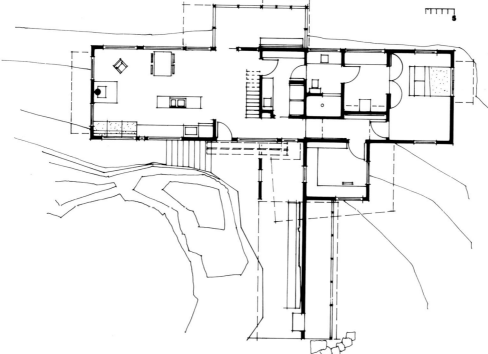

ARCHITECTURE AND JAZZ

THIS HOUSE FOR MUSICIANS explores the relationship of architecture and music in a lively, upbeat way. Architecture may be "frozen music," as Goethe said, but that observation offers little guidance in exactly how we translate musical ideas into built form. For that, we might look to the doctrine of musical figures, a theory about music developed in 1601 by Joachim Burmeister. Burmeister argued that music is analogous to language, with musical "figures" comparable to figures of speech. Music can rise or jump ahead or slide down. Buildings, too, contain "figures"—shapes, forms, patterns, textures—that can suggest such movement, and the orchestration of those elements can create a kind of visual music that engages the eye as much as sound does the ear.

In the Lutz house, David Salmela offers us a wholly compact composition of visual music. While barely more than one thousand square feet, the house presents a remarkable range of "figures." Salmela divides this composition into two parts: the bedroom wing has a nearly flat roof with bilateral symmetry, while the living-room wing sports an angled roof and numerous asymmetries. Here, then, stand the two dominant figures of architecture and music: the one orderly and calm, the other dynamic and restless.

Within these two larger figures, Salmela plays other melodic lines. The sleeping wing, which encloses the master bedroom on the first floor and a guest bedroom above, has a giant checkerboard pattern on its three elevations, composed of vertical battens painted white and flush panels painted dark. Against that overall rhythm, he creates a syncopated beat, with some windows large and centered on their checkerboard square, like giant whole notes, and other, smaller windows bridging between or sliding within the squares, like so many quarter notes.

In the adjacent daytime wing, this musical analogy starts to move in earnest. On the lakeside elevation, windows wide and narrow form a kind of musical line, dropping and ascending back to the same pitch. Meanwhile, hovering above them, a large, white-trimmed window seems to slide down the sloped roof, pushing against the lower bar of windows, which respond as if in improvisation.

That improvisation repeats itself on the land side of the house. There, a large and small window seem to slide down the roof pitch while sharing the same lintel. A piece of white-painted trim also angles down to the ground, recalling the form of the metronome. Elsewhere on that elevation, small windows scatter across the staff of the horizontal siding, like notes in a melody.

On the lake side of the house, the white-boarded railing of the entry porch stairs seems to arch up and then back down to become a fence that defines a deck. On the deck, the white-boarded back of a wide bench does its own arc into the air, interrupted by a notch that refers to the large window behind it. Between the house and the lake, the stone foundations and fireplace of the original structure on the site remain as an echo of the new house.

Inside, the musical ideas continue. A triangular balcony thrusts over the living room, echoing in plan the angle of the staircase and ceiling overhead and sounding a dominant note in the space. Likewise, the shelf along the living-room windows curves out to form a desk, echoing in plan the arch of the bench just outside and the rise and fall of the windows' pitch.

The Lutz house shows that architecture plays a kind of music that is anything but frozen. The swoops and slides, punctuations and pauses, and rises and falls of this house give us visual figures as active and engaging as those of any music. You can almost hear it.

TOP: THE BRIGHT COLOR AND BOLD FORMS OF THE LUTZ HOUSE CONTRAST WITH THE SURROUNDING WOODS. **MIDDLE:** A CHIMNEY FROM AN OLD CABIN VISUALLY BALANCES THE DYNAMIC MOVEMENT OF THE REAR OF THE HOME. **BOTTOM:** WITH ITS CONTRASTING HALVES, THE FRONT OF THE HOUSE HAS A STRONGLY RHYTHMIC QUALITY.

ABOVE: A STAIR, ECHOED IN THE ANGLED WINDOWS, LEADS TO THE SECOND-FLOOR BEDROOM. **RIGHT:** A PROWLIKE STUDY LOFT REFLECTS IN PLAN THE STEEP SLOPE OF THE ROOF OVERHEAD. **OPPOSITE:** THE INTERIOR FEATURES DISPLAY SPACE AND A CURVING DINING TABLE ALONG THE LAKESIDE WINDOWS.

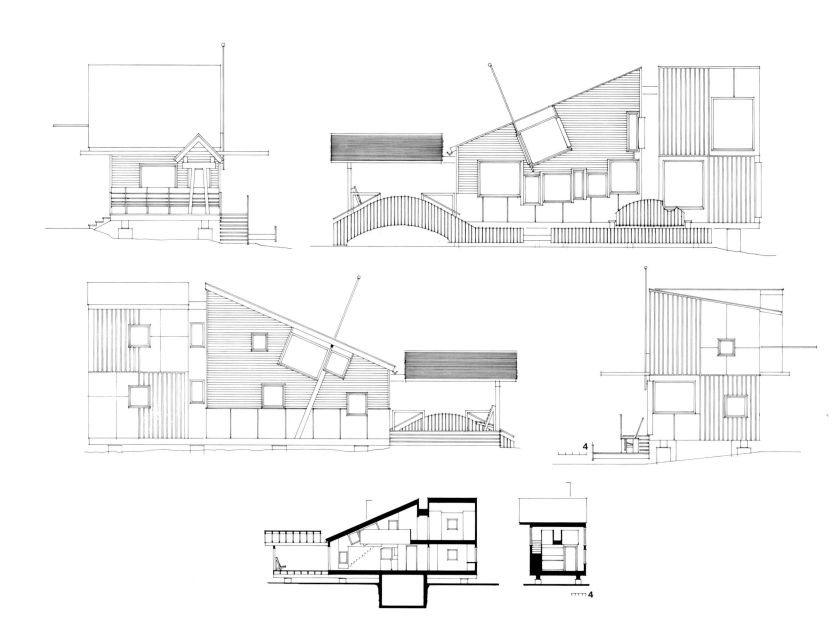

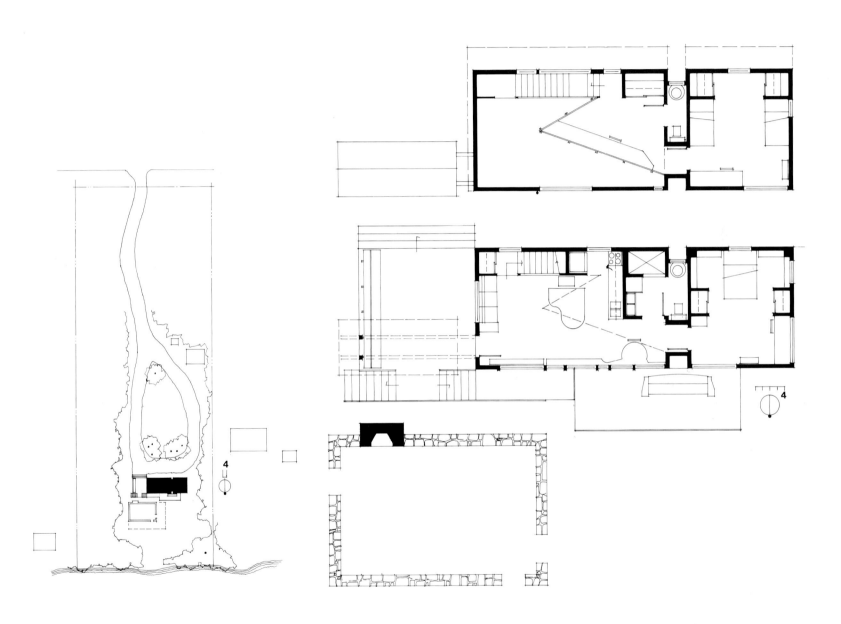

SYMMETRY AND ASYMMETRY

"THERE IS A FEARFUL SYMMETRY in the natural world," write ecologists John Reader and Harvey Croze in *The Pyramids of Life*, "an overwhelming order we are just beginning to understand." By symmetry they mean that, in the natural world, everything is in balance and that nothing is superfluous or goes to waste, with every plant and animal fitting into a food chain that either eats or is eaten, using whatever another animal leaves behind. At a time when humans need to find a better, more sustainable balance with the natural world, that notion of symmetry greatly affects the way in which we think about what we design and build.

Consider the idea of symmetry in David Salmela's designs for the residence and outbuildings he created for the Carlson family by their lake cabin. The house, which overlooks Lake Superior in a new subdivision in Duluth, differs from its "picturesque" neighbors by having a nearly complete, bilateral symmetry. Two single-car garages flank a central entry walk and sunken stone-walled garden, which leads to a central double-door entry, flanked by glass walls and highlighted overhead by a symmetrical row of shed-roof dormers. While we often think of such symmetry as formal, and in some sense opposed to the irregularity of nature, symmetry can also express a deeper harmony with nature. As is true of much vernacular architecture, the balance of elements in a building can reflect the balance of nature of which the structure is a part.

The Carlson house's forecourt, designed by landscape architects Shane Coen and Jon Stumpf, provides a microclimate, sheltered from the wind by the walls of the house and garages. The court's locally quarried stone walls and aspen trees also offer habitat for birds and small animals, representing a strong contrast to the monoculture lawns of the neighboring houses, with their near exclusion of other species. The symmetry of this forecourt does not look "natural"; it does not have undulating paths or picturesque placements of trees. Yet the geometry of the space represents the deeper order of the natural world, in which species seek a kind of balance with their environments and with each other.

Animals find ways to cohabit human environments if we give them half a chance, which is exactly what this garden does.

The symmetry repeats on the interior of the house, with bedrooms flanking a central family room on the lower level, living room and kitchen flanking a central dining room on the main level, and bedrooms flanking a central bath and dressing area on the upper level. As with the landscape, we still tend to think of asymmetry as more natural, more modern. But the "fearful symmetry" inside the Carlson house suggests that it applies to human nature as well as to the rest of the natural world. Humans, like all animals, seek to eliminate the superfluous and unnecessary, although in the developed world that has taken an unsustainable and paradoxical form, in which an ever more efficient economy encourages us to consume and discard ever larger amounts of materials and resources. Were we to see our behavior symmetrically, we would attend to where our trash goes as carefully as we attend to where our goods come from. The almost relentless symmetries of the Carlson house bring that to mind. For every space, there exists a parallel space; for every move, a related move. Symmetry in this sense represents not rigidity, but thoughts about the unseen parallels and unintended consequences of our actions.

The outbuildings Salmela designed for the Carlsons' lake cabin offer yet another way of looking at symmetry. The two long, narrow buildings, one devoted to equipment storage and the other to a shop, stand perpendicular to each other and form two sides of an outdoor space edged by the existing cabin and garage. The equipment-storage building has garage doors at either end and pass doors at the center of either side, with small square windows illuminating its length. The shop, in contrast, has three distinct parts: an unheated shop lit by the same small windows, a heated shop defined by two cross gables and illuminated by four large windows, and an outdoor covered space.

The one building has a single bilateral symmetry; the other, multiple local symmetries. A parallel of this, too, exists in nature. Modern agriculture, for example, has a single sym-

TOP: THE SYMMETRICAL FRONT OF THE CARLSON HOME CONTRASTS WITH THE ASYMMETRICAL DEVELOPER HOUSES NEARBY.
BOTTOM: LARGE, SWELLING COLUMNS AND A STRAIGHT STAIR DEMARCATE THE HALL FROM LIVING AREAS.

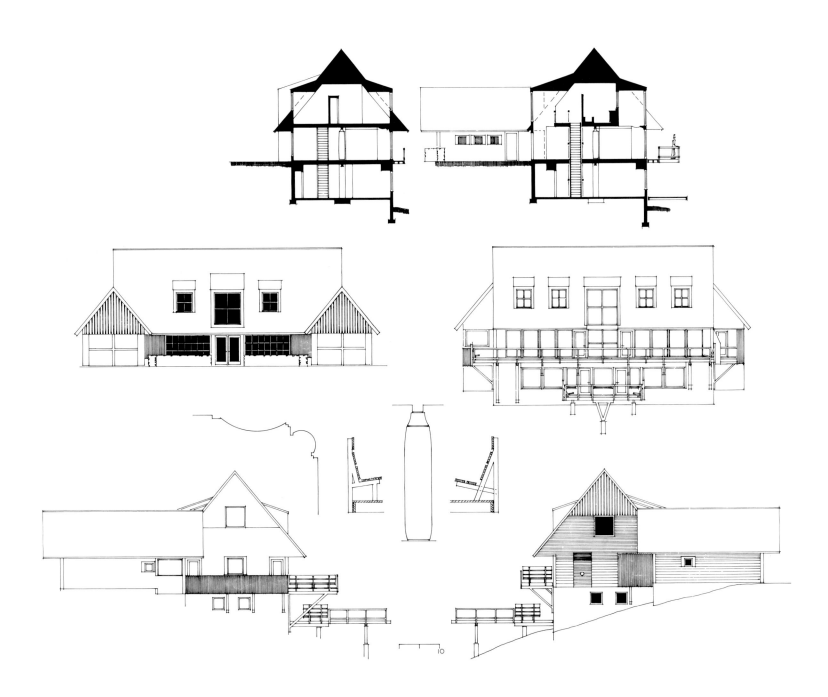

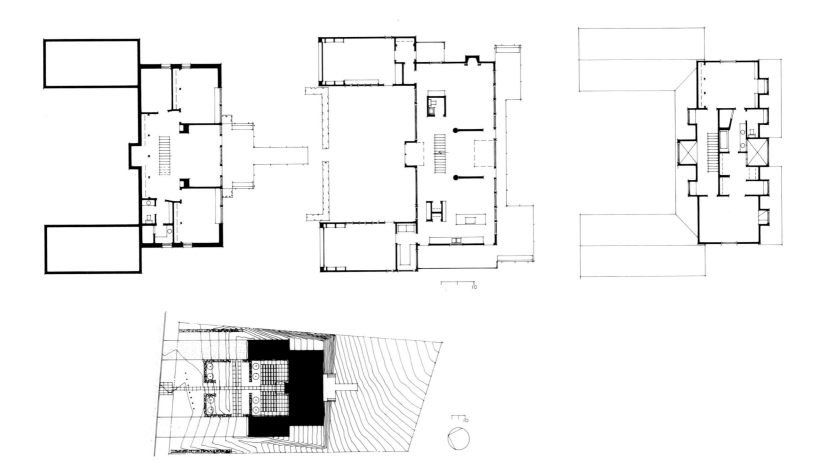

TOP: IN ITS VARIED ELEVATION, THE WORKSHOP REFLECTS ITS THREE DIFFERENT FUNCTIONS. **BOTTOM:** THE TWO OUTBUILDINGS FORM AN OUTDOOR SPACE WITH THE OWNER'S CABIN AND GARAGE.

metry, in which a dominant species edges out all others, creating an environment efficient to planting and harvest and yet vulnerable to pests. That utilitarian approach has its architectural equivalent in the single symmetry of the equipment shed, which is both efficient in its form and fenestration and also vulnerable as an unheated space.

Healthy ecosystems have a variety of species in many local symmetries, continually adjusting to each other and in various stages of thriving or declining. Less efficient in some ways, such environments are also highly adaptable, something no less true of the shop building. Its multiple symmetries represent diverse spaces—heated and unheated, indoors and out, bifurcated and not—that lend themselves to varied uses and offer greater adaptability than the singular space of the adjacent building.

The natural world may have a "fearful symmetry," but as this work shows, we have nothing to fear of symmetry in architecture. Indeed, were we to see symmetry in our buildings from an ecological perspective, we might begin to live in ways that would make the rest of nature perhaps less fearful of us.

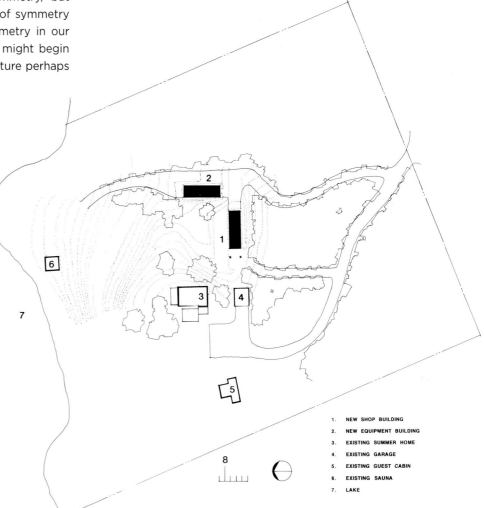

1. NEW SHOP BUILDING
2. NEW EQUIPMENT BUILDING
3. EXISTING SUMMER HOME
4. EXISTING GARAGE
5. EXISTING GUEST CABIN
6. EXISTING SAUNA
7. LAKE

WEATHER AND WEATHERING

WE GENERALLY THINK of the weather in two distinct ways. On one hand, we recognize the complex, interconnected flows of the natural world—the swirl of air masses, the rise and fall of temperatures and pressures, the transfers of electrical energy in storms. On the other hand, we reduce the complexity of weather to something quantifiable, measurable, mappable, so that we can make decisions about it.

That difference very much affects buildings, the structures we erect to protect us against the elements. Because of that protective role, most buildings reflect a reductionist view of weather, as their designers calculate such things as snow loads, air infiltration, and heat transfer through windows and walls. Such quantification plays a critical role in the design of buildings, but taken too far it becomes self-defeating, evident in the sealed-off, centrally heated and cooled cocoons within which we now often live and work. Reduced too far and quantified too much, the natural world comes to seem foreign to us—something we can exploit without seeing that the damage we do to it only damages ourselves.

Some architects have gone to the other extreme, expressing nature's flow and complexity with buildings that mimic that condition, with undulating and continuously morphing walls, floors, and roofs. While too literal to be much more than a symbolic gesture, this architecture of flow at least acknowledges the need to redress the balance in our relationship with nature. Another, more promising direction suggests that we see buildings as we do the weather itself, as something both distinct from and continuous with the energy flows around them. Buildings in this light would both protect us from and change with the seasons, creating their own microclimates and opening to the larger climate that surrounds them. The Webster house, designed by David Salmela when still with the firm Damberg, Scott, Peck, and Booker, suggests how that might be done.

The house, built for a retired couple on a lake in northern Minnesota, at first seems to recall the work of the Finnish architect Alvar Aalto. The single-sloped roof rising toward the sun and the walled outdoor patio on the south side bring to mind Aalto's own summerhouse on Muuratsalo Island. Likewise, the tall living room, with its stepped corner windows and its ability to be closed off from the rest of the house, recalls the residence Aalto designed for the Finnish composer Joonas Kokkonen.

The Webster house, though, transcends those specific architectural references. Perhaps because of the severity of the northern Minnesota climate, the house simultaneously resists and responds to the elements. Consider the form of the house. It hunkers down against the winter wind, with a low roof and nearly windowless north-facing façade. The laundry room, entry vestibule, main bathroom, and storage rooms run along the north side of the house, like an extra outer layer of clothing, protecting the living areas from the cold. The walled patio on the south further shelters the house from the cold winds that can blow off the adjacent lake, while a screened porch off the kitchen protects the owners from the onslaught of summer insects.

At the same time, the Webster house responds, both literally and figuratively, to its climate. Like the great masses of air that undulate horizontally and vertically around the globe, the main living spaces of the house provide a similar sense of wavelike flow. The kitchen opens to the den, which flows into the dining and living room, which opens to the loft and sleeping areas above, which overlook the walled patio, which flows back through the porch and into the kitchen. By offsetting each space from the next, Salmela provides undulating patterns of movement and rising and falling currents of air. He doesn't symbolize nature's complexity through form, but instead uses form to allow nature's complexity to occur.

At the same time, the house challenges our conception of the exterior wall as the sole barrier against the elements, a reflection of our resistance to the weather gone too far. Salmela establishes a range of temperature gradients throughout the house, depending upon the season. The wall enclosing the patio keeps out the wind and holds the sun's warmth, enabling it to be used later in the season than the typical exposed outdoor space. The south-facing glass

marks another temperature gradient, providing a warm zone inside the house, heating the main living spaces, at least in part, with the sun. In the depths of winter, another warm zone occurs at the back of the house, behind a curved screen that closes off the living room so that the owners do not have to heat such a large space. Meanwhile, in the summer, when air movement is most desired, the sleeping balcony that runs over the living and dining areas enables warm air to rise and cool air to enter off the lake and adjacent woods.

The Webster house is not a "solar" house in the narrow sense of that word. It doesn't tout an explicitly environmental agenda. And yet, in its understated way, the house shows how we can have a more balanced interaction with the weather around us, knowing when to resist and when to respond. Vernacular architecture, especially in cold climates, reflects that understanding; traditional Scandinavian log houses, for instance, had layers of space both inside the house and in the yard, whose use changed with the seasons. But such strategies have been largely forgotten, or purposefully ignored as being out-of-date.

In the Webster house, Salmela shows how we can usefully learn from the past without mimicking its forms. By understanding the principles that generated those forms, we can achieve the same goals in a more modern way. He also demonstrates here that we can live sustainably, in even the most extreme weather, by layering space, gradating temperatures, and adjusting uses. It's where the winds are blowing.

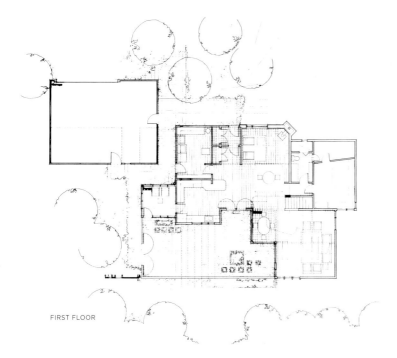

FIRST FLOOR

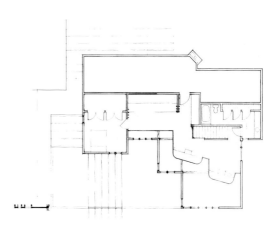

SECOND FLOOR

LIVING AND WORKING

OUR DIVIDING A DAY into working and all the rest—the eating, sleeping, and socializing that we call "living"—dates back only a couple of centuries. Before then, working and living intertwined over the course of a day, with tasks in the field or shop mixed with rest or repast, often in the same or nearby location. The Wick studio and house, another early project by David Salmela, represents a modern form of that premodern condition. Designed for a doll maker and her husband and elderly mother, the house shows how we might, once again, integrate living and working.

The house has two wings at slight angles to each other, with a tower connecting them. One wing consists of work space: a garage and receiving room on the first floor linked by a spiral stair to the doll-making studio above. The other "living" wing has the mother's room on the lower level, along with storage and utilities, and an upper level that contains living and dining space, a kitchen, library, bedroom, and bathroom. The tower encloses the entry and stair connecting the two wings, with an office on the third floor linked by a stair to the studio.

The organization of the house leads to a literal interweaving of activities over the day. The morning starts in the living wing and moves to the working wing, then moves back to the living wing at midday, back to the working wing in the afternoon, and ends in the living wing by day's end. The tower enables this with its dogleg stair, providing a physical connection and psychological separation between the two parts of the house.

Just as this house updates the idea of living and working in the same location, so too does it update a traditional form once taken by such environments. The client wanted a gambrel-roof house, which harks back to the barn vernacular of the region and to farm life, with its own type of live/work. Salmela has interpreted that desire in a way that seems old and new, premodern and modern, at the same time.

Unlike the bright red of the region's barns, this house has been painted an intense blue and green, which serves to integrate the structure into its wooded setting of deep green conifers and deciduous trees silhouetted against the bright blue skies of northern Minnesota. At the same time, he has made the gambrel roofs asymmetrical, with that of each wing skewed toward the other, as if to express the pull that living and working have on us as we move back and forth between them each day. The symmetrical gambrel roof of the tower serves as a kind of visual clamp, holding the two wings together symbolically as well as physically.

The windows in the house further this blurring between living and working, tradition and modernity. With their wide, white surrounds, the individual window units on the lower levels of the two wings run in continuous bands, like the horizontal strip windows of modern architecture reinterpreted in a vernacular form. Upstairs, the windows have the vertical proportion and transom lights of classical architecture, but are arranged in an asymmetrical and irregular way, as one might expect in a modern building in which the fenestration reflects the functions within. In both wings, the window surrounds have lintels and mullions that extend beyond the openings, recalling the exaggerated forms of some Scandinavian vernacular. The windows in the tower, in contrast, have thin surrounds and repetitive casements grouped in larger sections, like a vernacular interpretation of a modern curtain wall.

A more intimate scale may be one of the most important factors in being able to integrate living and working over the course of a day. The closer activities are in space, the easier we can connect them in time. Salmela achieves that intimacy of scale here through several means—sinking the "living" wing into the ground somewhat, bringing the gambrel-roof eaves down to within reach, lowering the upstairs window sills.

All of this seems particularly fitting for this house of a doll maker. It is through dolls that children first act out their roles as adults, going to work or making a home. And it is through architecture such as this that we can reimagine a life more intimate and more integrated than that which we have created as adults.

TOP: THE BRIGHT COLORS AND EXAGGERATED ROOF OF THE WICK RESIDENCE MAKE IT LOOK LIKE A DOLL'S HOUSE.
BOTTOM: A LONG LIVING AREA OCCUPIES ONE WING, A DOLL-MAKING STUDIO THE OTHER.

FACTS AND FICTION

BUILDINGS CONSIST OF FACTS: we can measure their dimensions, specify their materials, and list their functions. But such facts have meaning only according to the fictions we create about them. What dimensions we dictate, materials we call for, or functions we combine depend upon what we want to say with them, what story we want to tell through a building.

In the design of the Thompson house, David Salmela began with one such story, which evolved into another. The clients envisioned a traditional house fitting their extensive antique-furniture collection. The much beloved mid-twentieth-century Minnesota architect Edwin Lundie, known for his intimately scaled houses in American colonial and Scandinavian vernacular styles, became a reference. Salmela and the Thompsons visited many of the popular Lundie buildings and greatly respected his skillful hand, but found the interiors to be dark and overly detailed in an intentionally old-fashioned, Scandinavian way, without much alteration. So Salmela went back to the same sources Lundie looked at, analyzing the Scandinavian vernacular with the goal of making it modern at the same time. "I discovered," Salmela says, "that these buildings had a lot of light and were not overdone" in contrast to what he saw in Lundie's buildings.

So the story of the Thompson house began to change. Lundie's work embraced the Beaux-Arts fiction that a golden age existed in the past—rural Scandinavia—and that the modern world needed to recover that past, making as few changes as possible to update it. The fiction Salmela tells is not one of a golden age to which we should return, but of a modern era that had evolved from, and continuously altered, the past. He looks to Scandinavia's vernacular architecture not to copy it, but to learn its principles and interpret them for our time.

The Thompson house embodies that idea, with almost every fact about it driven by that evolutionary fiction. Its façade, for example, represents the notion of the modern having evolved from the vernacular. At one end of the house, a small, gable-roof wing containing a master bathroom has wide board-and-batten siding and narrow, divided-light casement windows. Although the wing was built at the same time as the rest of the house, the fiction places it as the "original" house to which the rest has been added. Reinforcing that notion, a somewhat larger (and, according to the fiction, somewhat later) section of the house adjoins the first, still vernacular in feel with the same form and surface but with somewhat larger windows illuminating the master bedroom's dressing area.

This evolutionary fiction continues along the façade. A classical, "eighteenth century" section, with the gable end to the street, much larger divided-light windows, and much narrower board-and-batten siding, comes next, followed by a "nineteenth-century" farmhouse section, complete with a shaped-board railing and a hipped dormer above a recessed entry. That is followed, in turn, by an homage to Lundie's early-twentieth-century work, with ganged windows, a more horizontal proportion, and oversized, shaped wood columns on either side of the front porch. Concluding this evolution is the "modern" two-car garage: asymmetrical, horizontal, large in scale. The house's white color, local symmetries, common materials, and unifying roofline visually tie this extraordinary evolution of styles together. It's as if Salmela were saying, *You want history? I'll give you history—all of it, in a row!*

The interior of the house continues the fiction. Classically arrayed, with columns framing a symmetrical fireplace and dormers letting in light from above, the living room has exposed columns, beams, and joists, and a flow of space on the upper level, all with a distinctly modern feel. The juxtaposition of the modern, the classical, and the vernacular occur elsewhere as well. The kitchen, for example, has a "modern" window framed by "traditional" wood columns.

In the Thompson residence, fiction is not extraneous to the building but essential to it. Every fact finds its place in the evolutionary story told through the house. While the story may be visual rather than literary, composed of real materials rather than imagined settings, the house makes the point that we literally cannot make architecture without creating fictions about it. And that's a fact.

TOP: THE THOMPSON HOUSE LOOKS AS IF IT HAD GROWN OVER TIME FROM AN OLD BOARDED COTTAGE.
BOTTOM: THE MAIN LIVING AREA, WITH ITS HEAVY TIMBER FRAME, SEEMS BOTH MODERN AND OLD.

ARCADIA AND UTOPIA

THE VILLA, as a building type, has long been associated with arcadia, an idealized vision of a golden age located in or close to nature. As Reinhard Bentmann and Michael Muller observe in their book *The Villa as Hegemonic Architecture*, the villa "repressed the social conflicts of the city . . . by focusing on a flight to the countryside." Most villas thus stand as large houses, commanding a spacious rural site and making allusions to either a classical or Gothic past.

If arcadia looks to an agrarian past and to escaping the conflicts of the city, utopias envision the opposite: ideal cities of the future, where the conflicts of today get resolved through economic, political, and social change. Bentmann and Muller polarize these two approaches, seeing arcadia as the conservative reaction to utopian progress and the villa as the embodiment of antiprogressive trends.

David Salmela's design of the Unger-Sonnerup house suggests a different interpretation of the arcadian and utopian traditions. At first glance, the house seems to adhere closely to the villa type. It makes several references to Scandinavian classicism, with its long, gabled form, vertical white siding, tall transom windows, and central ornamental porches. It has an interior of symmetrically arranged rooms grouped around a grand double stair. And it commands a view over a broad back lawn framed by trees.

On closer inspection, though, the house also raises questions about the villa as a building type. While the back of the house appears to sit in an arcadian landscape, its front has an almost urban character, with a circular auto court flanked by a pair of garages, like the central square of some nascent village. Rather than represent just an escape from the city, the villa can also promote urbanism where it didn't exist before. The open interior of the Unger-Sonnerup house suggests yet another interpretation of arcadia. While it has often served as an ideal for a privileged elite, arcadia has also shared with utopian thought the idea of community, enhanced by a common focus at its center and a clear boundary around its edge. Arcadia may be the flip side of utopia, but both engage the same coin.

As so often happens in Salmela's work, the embrace of opposites works in more than one direction. The Unger-Sonnerup house raises questions not only about arcadia but about utopia as well, especially the utopia represented by modern architecture and its radical revisioning of domestic life. Salmela, for example, places the kitchen on axis with the main entrance, at the center of the back of the house—a privileged position that expresses the importance of technology in modern life and of sharing the work within the household. And yet a cutout crown evocative of Scandinavian royalty hangs above the kitchen, with all of its high-tech, laborsaving equipment. It reminds us that we cannot have a future without a past, utopia without arcadia.

Salmela also groups the main living spaces at either end of the house, with multiple doors allowing a flow of circulation akin to a modernist "free plan." Here, the balance between old and new treads a fine line. The plan, open enough to feel modern, also has just enough closure to recall the enfilade arrangement of rooms in a classical building. It may be that the boundary between tradition and modernity is not a gulf, but the finest line.

The Unger-Sonnerup house suggests that we draw that line, not between past and future, nature and city, arcadia and utopia, but instead between those who would dichotomize such matters and those who would have them coexist. The latter is a larger group than we might think. Despite the efforts of its polemicists to separate it from what had come before, modern architecture also represented an attempt at conjoining arcadia and utopia evident in the many modernist buildings that stand in bucolic landscapes. From that perspective, the utopian City on the Hill seems compatible with the arcadian Garden of Eden. That has been particularly true in the United States, a country founded on the utopian urge for an egalitarian future within an arcadian landscape of abundant nature. Such a vision, however flawed it might be in practice, has drawn immigrants to these shores for centuries and still finds its echo in projects such as this.

TOP: THE UNGER-SONNERUP HOUSE LORDS OVER ITS SITE, SUGGESTING BOTH A DOMINANCE OF AND CONNECTION TO NATURE.
BOTTOM: THE EXTERIOR INTENTIONALLY RECALLS THE SWEDISH COUNTRY HOUSE WITH ITS ORNAMENTED PORCHES.

RIGHT: SKYLIGHTS ILLUMINATE THE CENTER OF THE HOUSE AND THE STAIRS TO THE MAIN FLOOR. **BOTTOM:** THE KITCHEN HAS AN ENTRY SURROUND SUGGESTIVE OF A CROWN, WITH PAIRED STAIRS BEHIND.

The coexistence of past and future does not mean we must necessarily harmonize them. As the Unger-Sonnerup house shows, with its arcadian elevations and siting harkening the past and its utopian plans and details looking to the future, those two traditions often occupy different, if related, realms. But out of their coexistence comes a vitality and openness characteristic of this country—and of this country villa.

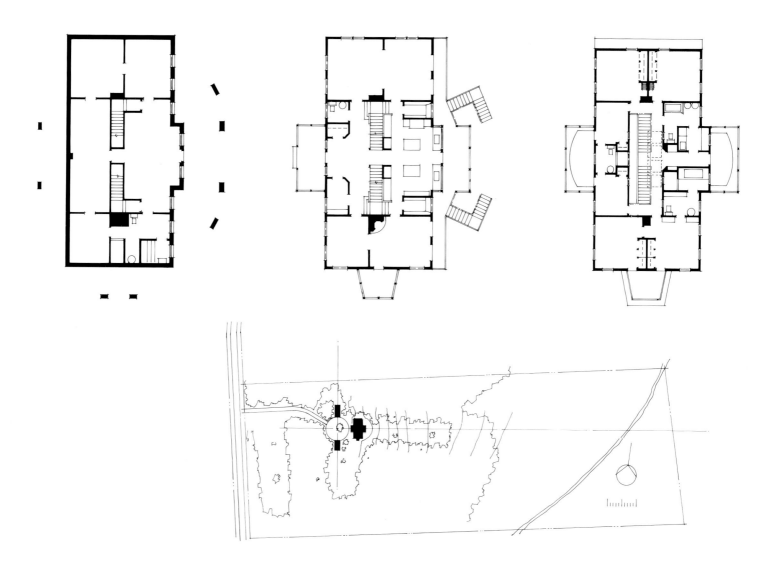

RECREATION AND RE-CREATION

ALTHOUGH NOW MAINLY RECREATION, cross-country skiing once served as a major form of transportation in Scandinavia. One of the largest cross-country ski meets in the United States occurs annually in Mora, Minnesota, and the ski center that David Salmela designed for it speaks to the way in which new forms can help re-create old ones.

The gabled ski center looks, at first glance, like a traditional villa you still find in rural Sweden. The building has a central two-story block, with one-story wings extending asymmetrically to either side and with repetitive square windows that amply illuminate the interior. Inside, a central lobby and second-floor lounge separate the two wings, which contain restrooms, lockers, saunas, and showers.

This is a modern building with a seemingly nonmodern expression. But just as modern transportation has let cross-country skiing become a sport, and at its most extreme an art form, so too do modern functions in buildings such as this let old forms take on new life and new meaning, especially when they become an exaggerated form of their former selves.

This is at work in the way Salmela deals with the building's major architectural elements. He exaggerates the size of the windows and their surrounds, both of which are functionally unnecessary but all the more important as an expression of the size and drama of the outdoor races that occur there. The form of the building has a similar exaggeration: longer, lower, and simpler than a traditional vernacular villa, in the same way that modern

cross-country skis have simplified and extended their historic form. Likewise, the interiors of the ski center, wrapped in naturally finished wood, no longer need such wood surfaces, which is why their use here signifies the connection of such skiing back to a time when it was central to people's mobility in snowbound lands.

Recreation has become a dominant characteristic of contemporary life, with its physical activity compensating for the physical inactivity of modern work. And just as we "re-create" the body through the exercise of muscles we may no longer use, we have come to re-create, through buildings such as this ski center, the exaggerated memories of a past lost but not forgotten. Some may find such architectural "re-creations" superficial, but, like all recreation, they serve a healthy, and ultimately profound, purpose.

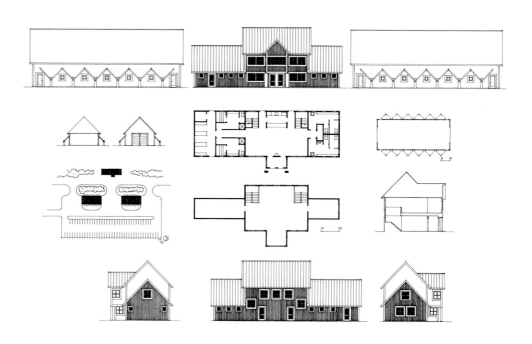

TOP: THE SIMPLE FORMS AND BRIGHT COLOR OF THE MORA VASALOPPET NORDIC SKI CENTER SIGNAL THE SKIERS' DESTINATION.
BOTTOM: THE SKI-WAXING ROOM REPEATS THE WOOD-LINED INTERIORS OF THE CABINS AROUND NEARBY LAKES.

ADAPTATION AND COMPLEXITY

WE HUMANS, like all organisms, adapt to our environment, but unlike most other species, we also adapt our environment to us, through the construction of buildings and the alteration of the land. The apparent complexity of this process seems almost impossible to comprehend, but geneticist John Holland, in his book *Hidden Order*, has identified seven principles that underlie the adaptive behavior of all species and that apply to our alteration of the physical environment. That is evident to varying degrees in almost every building, and particularly apparent and elegantly applied in this small, 1,800-square-foot house that David Salmela designed for his longtime carpenter, Rod Holmes, and his wife, Joan, on a spacious site in northern Minnesota along the St. Louis River.

The first adaptive principle, says Holland, is aggregation, where the collection of simple things creates a larger and more complex whole. Aggregation underlies the very idea of the Holmes house, patterned after a collection of small cabins Rod Holmes remembers as a boy. The house consists of a collection of square modules. The main part of the house has three modules, containing a master bedroom, living room, and kitchen/dining room, offset in plan. A corridor connects the main house to a guest wing containing a living room and sleeping room in two aligned modules. The guest wing is connected by another corridor to a garage and gun room, also occupying two modules end-to-end. The aggregation of modules creates a varied composition of white gable-roofed forms, which cluster around three sides of an entry court defined by a white fence. The result of this assemblage of modules looks more like a small village than a single house, reinforcing Holland's claim that adaptation occurs best through the mutual cooperation of individuals: in this case, the cooperation of a family.

A second adaptive principle—tagging—involves identifying like and unlike things and sorting them into larger categories. At the Holmes house, you see this strategy of differentiation used in many ways. The gable roofs of the main house orient in one direction, while that of the guesthouse orient in another; the ceilings of the main house curve, while those of the guesthouse and garage don't; the main

living areas are identified by lap siding, while the secondary or servant spaces have board-and-batten wainscots; the linking corridors have gable roofs, while the entry vestibule and rear-door trellis have curved tops. In visually identifying elements of the house in this way, Salmela helps us make sense of its various parts. At the same time, he uses forms and materials associated with home, one of the most powerful adaptive environments humans have.

Nonlinearity constitutes a third adaptive strategy, where complexity results from simple, geometrical relationships. Consider the kitchen, which serves not only for food preparation, but also as a dining room, a work space, a passageway, and an entry closet. Multiple activities thus occur in a single, eighteen-foot-square space. And the squareness of the space matters here. As in nonlinear equations, whose simplicity disguises the complexity of their results, architecture that has relatively simple dimensional relationships in plan, such as squares or golden-section rectangles, can generate much greater complexity of use than structures with highly particular shapes or fragmented floor plates.

Holland defines flows, a fourth adaptive strategy, by the number of nodes and connectors in a system, something also amply evident in the Holmes house. At every transition point from one module to the next, you have at least two directions in which you can travel. This leads to what Holland calls the "multiplier effect," in which something simple creates multiple options. In the case of the Holmes house, that multiplier effect leads to the appearance of greater space than actually exists. The other aspect of flow—what Holland calls the "recycling effect"—comes from doubling back along networks and nodes, as happens in the Holmes house when you move back through each module to retrace your steps. The lack of internal corridors in the main house, although it may provide less privacy, does allow for more flexibility, and with it more adaptability.

Adjoining rooms also enhance interaction, which Holland sees as fundamental to the adaptive principle of diversity. Single-use rooms off a hallway not only have limited function, but they inhibit the interaction of people. At the Holmes house, each room becomes a center of diverse

TOP: THE HOLMES FARMSTEAD'S SERIES OF WHITE GABLE-ROOF STRUCTURES RECALL THE LOCAL CABINS.
BOTTOM: THE PARTS OF THE HOUSE SURROUND AN ENTRY COURT, ENCLOSED BY A BOARD FENCE.

VAULTED WOOD CEILINGS HAVE A CABIN FEEL AND EMPHASIZE THE SPACE OF EACH ROOM.

activities, suggesting—as in so much of Salmela's work—that the modern notion of an open plan may work best when mixed with its opposite: a traditional room plan, where clear boundaries allow for greater interaction.

The last two adaptive strategies that Holland finds in nature—models and building blocks—also have a presence here. Nature builds models to predict the future, using a few simple building blocks that, when combined, form almost infinite complexity. At the Holmes house, the single-room cabin became a model able to accommodate a variety of functions. And just as nature eliminates details so that the important ideas of a model emerge, so too has

Salmela reduced the "cabin" to its essential features as a square, gabled white form. With that as a building block, he then played with it, cutting into it at the guesthouse living room, adding to it at the trellised patio, and extruding it as the garage.

Such formal moves are anything but arbitrary. They show that we design as we live, using the same seven strategies in adapting our environment to us as we use in adapting to it. In this sense, even the simplest work of architecture—as the Holmes house attests—can remind us of the most fundamental aspects of who we are and how we might continue to sustain ourselves on the earth.

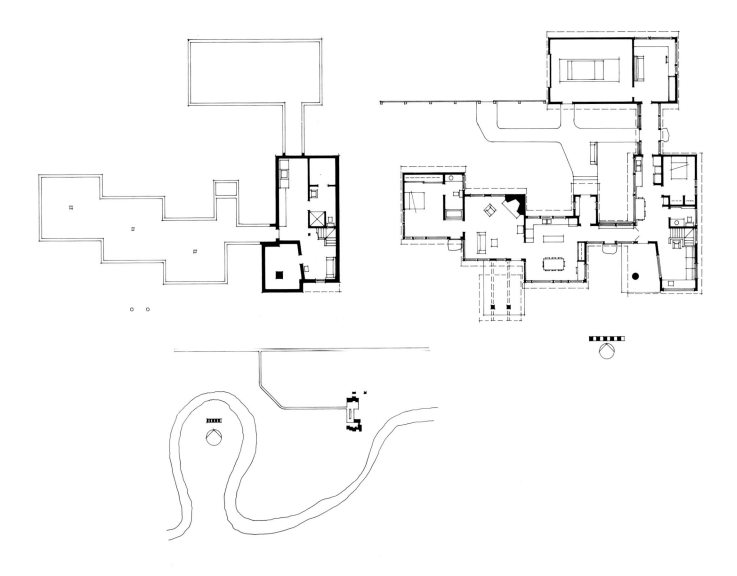

SIZE AND SCALE

WE THINK OF SIZE as something absolute, easily measured and readily agreed upon, and yet size is also completely relative, a matter of one thing's relation to another. Architects deal with size all the time, needing to dimension almost everything in the buildings we design. But we mostly deal with matters of scale, with the relation of one size to another, and in so doing we help people understand their relation to the world and to each other.

The Holmes house, which David Salmela designed for Brad Holmes, his frequent carpenter, exemplifies that idea. Starting with a partly built house, Salmela redesigned it in ways that emphasize differences in scale, playing with our expectations of what is large and small. For example, the house is small relative to the average home, with a single, large living, dining, and kitchen space on the main floor and a narrow stair leading to a small bedroom and large bathroom on the second floor. But the house, especially from the lakeside, has an unexpectedly large scale. A flat gable end spans the entire width of the back of the house, presiding over a two-story-high glass wall divided into small rectangular windows that make it hard to tell where one floor ends and the other begins. This makes the house look larger than it is.

Salmela plays a different kind of game on the front of the house, which seems grand and diminutive at the same time. A broad shed roof, for example, rakes back to a series of square windows, whose small size creates a forced perspective that makes the shed roof seem longer than it is. At the same time, the wide, flat gable above those windows looks closer than it is, countering the apparent distance. The same uncertainty of scale occurs along the front porch, where oversized round columns frame two large living-room windows, divided into smaller lights, and a smaller vestibule window next to them, divided into four large lights. While the vestibule window stands forward of the living-room windows, the jump in scale exaggerates the difference. That also occurs above, where a large window in the dormer clerestory above the entry contrasts with the small second-floor windows behind it, making them seem much farther back than they are.

The changing scale of this house gives it a refreshing playfulness with a serious intent. The house reminds us that everything depends upon keeping things in proper scale and not thinking of ourselves as larger than we are, or the world as smaller than it is.

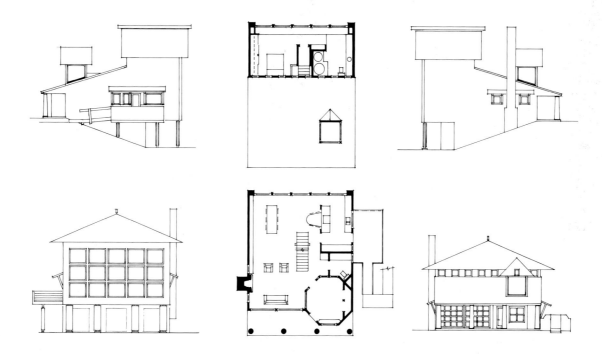

THE PLAY OF SCALES IN THE HOLMES RESIDENCE IS EVIDENT IN THE WINDOWS, WHICH SEEM EITHER TOO BIG OR TOO SMALL.

CAR AND HOUSE

OUR HOMES have long been a reflection of who we are, but over the past one hundred years, so have our cars, evident in the amount of space we devote to housing them and the prominent place we put them, with wide driveways to the street. Rarely, though, do the houses we construct for our cars—our garages—match the expressive quality of the vehicles inside.

An exception is the stand-alone, two-car garage and adjacent workshop that David Salmela designed for the Leakes. Adjacent to their existing house, this small structure—a building type that most architects pass up as too tiny—brings into high relief the convergence of house and car. A taut surface of horizontal bands of shingles clad the flat-roofed building, giving it a sleekness and sense of movement that recall the lines and motion of an automobile. Likewise, the workshop, offset from and slightly in front of the two-car garage, recalls the way in which cars often sit in driveways, slightly askew. The combination of a minimalist exterior and visually active interior that you see in most cars also finds a parallel here, presenting a fairly blank face to the road with the garage doors closed and a brightly lit, somewhat evocative interior with them open.

From the side facing the house and from the backyard, the garage and workshop do an about-face, becoming more homelike and less carlike. A wood-framed porch wraps around the back of the workshop, providing a covered place toward the house and an outdoor place in which to sit or work. Repeating square windows and a hip roof that terminates in a south-facing skylight also give the workshop a homey feel. At the same time, the garage presents a blank wall to the backyard, as if the two parts of this structure were like a yin and yang, one facing frontward and the other backward.

That two-sidedness seems fitting for the two enclosures in which we spend most of our time, our house and our car. Our cars have become like homes to us, places in which we invest psychologically, however poor a financial investment they make. But we have yet to become equally invested in the homes we build for our cars, the garages that some spend considerable time in but that rarely rise, like the Leake workshop, to the level of architecture.

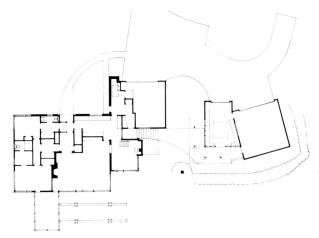

ABOVE: IN THE BACK, THE WORKSHOP OPENS TO A PORCH AND UP TO A CLERESTORY IN THE PEAKED ROOF. **OPPOSITE TOP:** THE EXPOSED FRAMING, SKYLIGHT, AND WINDOWS ALL AROUND GIVE THE LEAKE WORKSHOP AN AIRY FEEL. **BOTTOM:** THE FAÇADE OF THE WORKSHOP HAS AN ABSTRACT QUALITY, WITH UNORNAMENTED VOLUMES AND A PYRAMIDAL ROOF.

BOUNDARIES AND OVERLAPS

ARCHITECTURE can create conceptual as well as physical boxes around us, leading us to assume that everything in life should neatly fit the containers we construct for them. The Aas house, which David Salmela designed with his then business partner Cheryl Fosdick, might cause us to question that assumption. In both its form and detail, the house expresses the idea that nothing ever entirely fits the boundaries we draw around them, and that life is a series of overlaps and intersections from which new life grows.

You get a sense of that from the moment you see the Aas house. What looks like the end of a gable roof turns out to be a wall extending up from inside the house, while next to it two half-gables stand at ninety degrees to one another, as if formerly one roof is now split in two. The unusual rooftop sends a signal that nothing here is entirely what it seems or fits neatly into our assumptions about it.

The entry to the house reinforces that sensibility. From the drive, you proceed under a steep gable roof—this one whole and intact—along a retaining wall and into an outdoor court. What looked like it will take you inside puts you back out. The front door, contrary to what you might expect, turns its back to the entrance passage, forcing you to look for the door around the corner of a projecting vestibule to see how to get in.

Once you are inside, nothing seems to align with the exterior. The wall of the vestibule, angled in plan, directs you back along the angled wall of the entry hall to the angled kitchen counter framed by two angled walls, creating a sense of movement within the rectilinear plan. An angled skylight above the living room, dining room, and study suggests another way of breaking out of a box, with ceiling planes overlapping and not aligned with the walls below. Another sort of overlap occurs at the master bedroom, where the bathroom and closet stand within the larger living-room block and also within the rectangle of the bedroom. And making the point even more emphatically, the roof edge, beams, and joists extend beyond the exterior walls along the south and west sides, providing shade from the sun but also reminding us, through the architecture, that life is full of overlaps and that nothing ever entirely aligns.

ABOVE: THE AAS HOUSE FEATURES A SERIES OF ARCHITECTURAL FRAGMENTS, EVIDENT IN THE VARIOUS ROOF FORMS.
OPPOSITE: THE HOUSE'S VARIOUS FACES OFFER DIFFERENT VIEWS OF LAKE SUPERIOR.

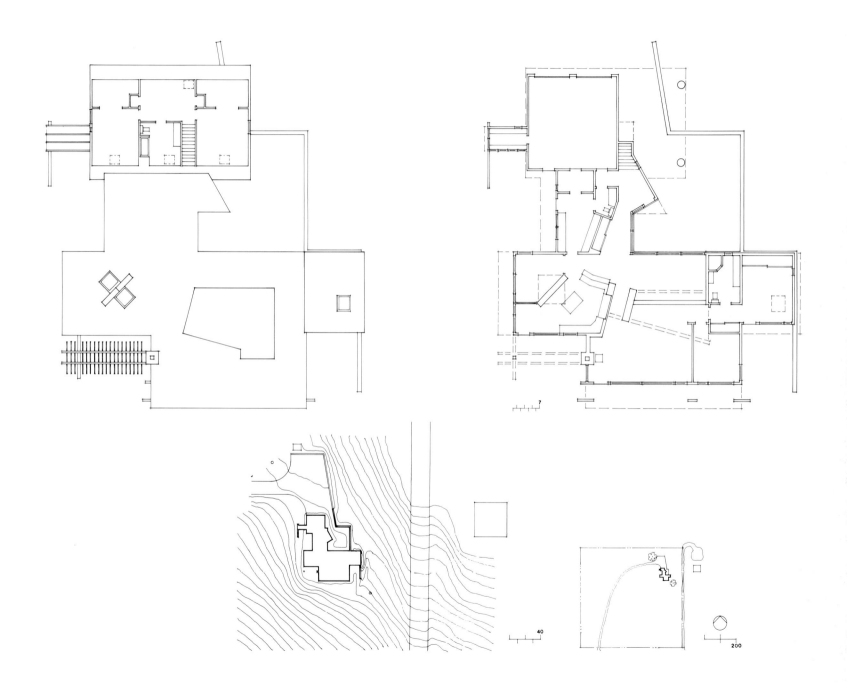

40

7

200

MOTION AND STASIS

IN THIS HOUSE for his brother Lyle and sister-in-law Elaine, David Salmela explores one of the paradoxes of modern architecture: its fascination with movement in an otherwise static medium. Ever since beginning to think of buildings as analogous to machines, architects have sought to make these heavy structures look light. We go to great lengths to prevent buildings from actually moving, and yet some among us want them to look like they do, to the point where their fixed metal or glass skins seem almost to flap in the wind.

The Salmela house, while not as literal about the expression of movement as some of today's architecture, conveys a sense of movement in several ways. As you approach the house, the garage twists slightly away from the main house, and the wide eaves on this north face look as if the shed roofs had slightly slid off the walls. For David Salmela, the countering of our expectations almost always comes with a bit of wit and a wink of the eye.

The sense of things sliding continues around the sides and back of the house. On the south face, horizontal and vertical sunscreens slip past the windows they shade, with stepped or curved faces that seem to dance along the back elevation. Meanwhile, two skylights on the main roof of the house angle toward the sun, as if reaching up to catch its rhythms.

Inside, the sense of motion continues, with a series of largely glazed walls on the upper floor stepping back toward the west, as if having telescoped from one another, craning to see the sunset. The suggestion of movement also occurs with the angled walls of the bedrooms on the lower level, the

angled ends of the outdoor decks, and the angled screen wall that divides the lower family room.

Machines move, but so do the sun and the seasons, and the exterior of the Salmela house suggests that responding to the latter may, in this more ecologically minded era, be a better direction for architecture to go. So too do people move, and the interior of the Salmela house shows how architecture can angle along with us as we go about our chores over the course of a day. Architecture has long been a kind of static foil to our motion, but when buildings move with us and for us, as happens here, we can be moved by them.

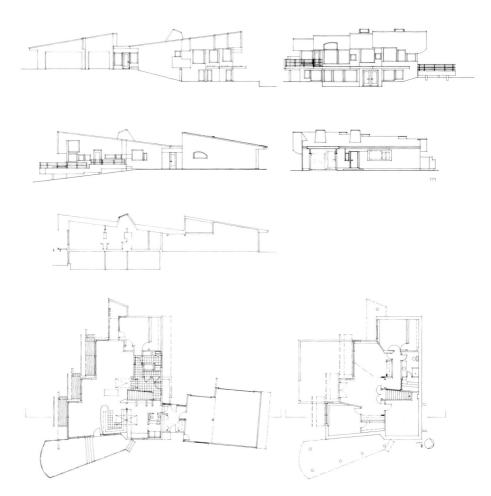

IN THE SALMELA HOUSE, MOVEMENT IS EVIDENT IN THE SCREEN WALLS, BALCONIES, AND SUNSHADES THAT SLIP PAST EACH OTHER.

MEDIA AND ARCHITECTURE

POSTMODERNISM has meant many different things, from a renewed interest in context and history to a new-found respect for diversity and subjectivity, to a newly acquired understanding of media and its effect on our lives. All of those meanings emerge in David Salmela's Wilson house, perhaps his most explicitly postmodern project, designed at a time when that movement was in full flower.

Consider the house in relation to its context. Standing on a hill overlooking Lake Vermilion in northern Minnesota, the L-shaped structure has a pair of garages that form an entry court, partly enclosed by a board fence. The whole looks like a composition of small houses, such as those found in the old mining towns in the area. The house's two wings also echo the region's characteristic architecture: tall, narrow structures with gable roofs perpendicular to the street and rear shed-roof lean-tos. The gabled offset garages bring to mind as well the region's many small lakeside cabins, the primitive hut that so enamored postmodernists.

For all of its supposed rejection of modernism, however, postmodernism retained the modernist concern for historical evolution. You see that in the way Salmela treats the Wilson house's allusions to the past. The gable roofs, for example, are steeply pitched in the local vernacular, but they also have flat, triangular tympanums, echoing the Euclidean geometries of modernism. Likewise, the divided windows, recalling the double-hung windows of worker housing, have an exaggerated size and simplicity that ensure no one would mistake them as old. Such elements signal the newness of the house. They also show how much the evolution of architecture has been toward a media-driven view of the world, where the flat, simplified forms of television, film, and photography have come to be seen as real to us as the three-dimensional world these media record.

The postmodern interest in diversity and subjectivity also finds expression in the Wilson house. The house has a fairly straightforward plan, with a central living room flanked by a master-bedroom suite on one side and a dining/kitchen/service wing on the other. An office occupies the second floor of one wing; a bedroom, the other. The various spaces in the house take diverse forms. Some have a modernist character, such as the great room, with its high shed-roof opening up to the view. Others have a more classical feel, such as the dining room, with its exedra allowing light down from the second-floor windows. Still others have a "deconstructed" quality, such as the tall screened porch, with its inverted ridge that seems to collapse into the space. As in the postmodern conception of contemporary life, the house breaks down into a series of fragments, each coherent in itself but juxtaposed in unexpected ways to create a diverse whole.

Such diversity generates a subjectivity of a particular kind. Postmodernism acknowledges the subjective basis of all actions, although it also embraces the idea that what we do is part of a larger social and cultural context. That tension between the subjective and the socially determined gives the Wilson house a dynamic quality. The house's quirky details and idiosyncratic window arrangements enhance the sense of subjective freedom at work in Salmela's design, while the house's overall form and vernacular character emphasize the determining role of local culture. In postmodern life, where the media often defines our sense of reality, the private and the public, the subjective and the objective, and freedom and constraint all tend to blur.

In architecture, the media has had an especially visible effect on reality. Because architecture is immobile and geographically dispersed, architects know about most buildings through the drawings and photographs of them in books and magazines, which define the context and culture of the field. How architects respond to that visual context in turn defines where they stand within the design culture. In the Wilson house, Salmela takes a decidedly eclectic position. He treats the building as "a premodern building designed in a postmodern time," alluding to the architecture of Gunnar Asplund, whose early-twentieth-century buildings have a similar archaic and eclectic character.

Yet the house also refers to the work of more recent architects. The wavy slat screen, shielding the great room's tall, south-facing windows from the sun, recalls the light

TOP: THE WILSON HOUSE BLENDS INTO ITS CLASSIC MINNESOTA SETTING: AMONG TREES, BY A LAKE, IN THE SNOW. **MIDDLE:** VIEWED FROM LAKE VERMILION, THE HOUSE LOOKS LIKE A COLLECTION OF WATERFRONT COTTAGES. **BOTTOM:** WHILE THE TALL, NARROW HOUSE FORMS LOOK OLD, THEIR FLATNESS REFLECTS THEIR MODERNITY.

ABOVE: WITH ITS INVERTED GABLE, THE SCREENED PORCH RECALLS THE EARLY WORK OF FRANK GEHRY. **OPPOSITE:** SLATS BENDING UNDER THEIR OWN WEIGHT ADD A "FALSE" CEILING TO THE LIVING ROOM.

lattice walls with which Charles Moore sometimes wrapped his buildings. The screened porch, with its tall, boxlike form and inverted ridge, brings to mind the early Southern California work of Frank Gehry. The large, divided square windows on the south face echo the childlike fenestration popularized by Robert Venturi and Denise Scott Brown. And the triangular pediments and round oculus windows on the north façade borrow from the abstract historicism of Aldo Rossi.

The range of visual references here makes the point that, in this postmodern era, choice matters more than consistency. If another architect advances something of use, why not employ it? The skill comes in making such varied sources cohere into a composition, and here Salmela succeeds brilliantly. While the Wilson house borrows media images from Italy to Los Angeles, it manages to make them work in a building that also seems quite at home by a lake in northern Minnesota—a feat, in itself, worthy of media attention.

DAVID SALMELA'S work continues unabated, with myriad projects in design or under construction as this book goes to press. Like the completed buildings shown here so far, his new work embraces apparently contradictory ideas with forms that seem at once large and small, light and heavy, inhabited and ruinous. But this new work also pursues fresh and innovative directions as an outgrowth of what has come before.

The geography of the work, for example, has begun to expand, with projects now in places such as St. Louis and the California coast. Physical dispersal presents a challenge to an architect whose work has, up to now, largely rooted itself in the Scandinavian culture of the northern Midwest. The projects farther afield certainly have great power and presence, suggesting that Salmela's architecture is more rooted in a set of ideas and a way of working than in a particular region of the country. But they also represent a change in the forms he has commonly used in the past.

That raises a second area of expansion, in the aesthetics of the work. Despite the postmodern character of much of his built work, Salmela says that he remains a modernist in his own mind—an embrace of apparent opposites very much in keeping with his architecture. The modernist in him has begun to have a greater impact on the form of his buildings, and increasingly projects have shallow sloped roofs, a feature that he correctly attributes to the saving of money. Likewise, he has begun to use more frequently such characteristically modernist features in his buildings as strip windows, parallel bearing walls, and upper stories that appear to float above glassy first floors.

All of this, though, retains the character that makes Salmela's work so appealing. There is no moralistic modernism here. Instead, he continues to surprise us with wit, designing buildings that seem to play a part of some pretend, fictional world. In one project, the gable roof looks like an imaginary fallen tree has dented it. In another, the guesthouse looks like it has slid out from the main house, as if wanting a little privacy. In a third, the part of the house that bridges the more public and private quarters becomes, literally, a bridge between them, as if crossing some imaginary river of space.

The power of David Salmela's architecture lies in the contradictions it embraces, the stories it tells, and the wit it uses in the telling. Other architects can tell other public fictions and embrace other apparent opposites. But from the evidence of Salmela's built work as well as his pending projects, there is no question that somewhere in such an approach greatness lies.

WORKS | IN PROGRESS

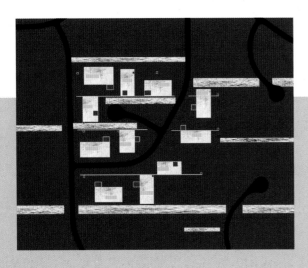

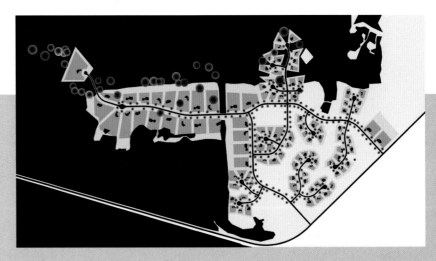

ABOVE: THE DEVELOPMENT'S ROADS WIND AMONG THE TALL GRASS, WINDBREAKS, AND FENCES TO ACCESS EACH HOUSE PLOT.

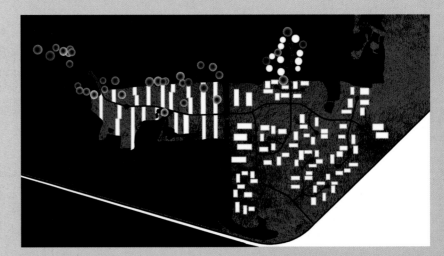

RIGHT TOP TO BOTTOM: THE ROADS FOR A CLUSTERED CUL-DE-SAC DEVELOPMENT FOR MAYO WOODLANDS HAD ALREADY BEEN INSTALLED BY THE TIME COEN + PARTNERS TOOK ON THE PROJECT. THE NEW SCHEME PUTS HOUSE LOTS IN RECTANGLES OF GRASS MOWED OUT OF TALL PRAIRIE GRASS. WINDBREAKS OF DOUBLE AND TRIPLE ROWS OF TREES AND LINES OF FENCES CONNECT THE HOUSE PLOTS.

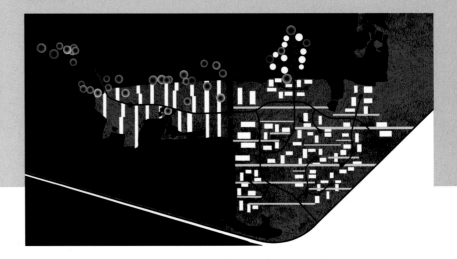

THE BIOMORPHIC AND THE ORGANIC

THE CURVILINEAR STREETS and cul-de-sacs of the suburb began with the best of environmental intentions: adapting the infrastructure of a place to its existing contours. However, over time the winding roads and dead-end circles became not just a cliché that had nothing to do with the lay of the land, but a clever way of cramming in more houses on a site with pie-shaped lots.

This shift in the original intent of the curvilinear street paralleled a change in the way we think about the "organic." While the term has acquired an aesthetic meaning related to the biomorphic shapes and irregular forms of nature, the organic originally had two different meanings. For Aristotle, the organic had a zoological reference to the body as an integrated system of parts, while for Goethe it had a botanical reference to the process of growing plants. Those earlier ideas have new relevance in this age of environmental awareness. And there is no better example of that than Mayo Woodlands, a 220-acre residential development in Rochester, Minnesota, designed by landscape architects Coen + Partners, with houses by David Salmela and Timothy Alt.

Mayo Woodlands marks an important shift in the way we think of the organic, representing a move away from its superficial analogy to biomorphic shapes and toward a new conception of it, based on its older meanings. Occupying former farmland, meadows, and woods owned by the Mayo family, the development began with the Rochester engineering firm McGhie and Betts laying out a conventional, curvilinear suburban development. One of the members of the Mayo family, however, did not want a conventional development and hired Coen + Partners to design something that might serve as a national model for innovative residential development. Shane Coen, in turn, hired Altus Architecture and Salmela Architect.

Accepting the curving road system already in place, Coen overlaid the former fields and meadows with five-foot-high native prairie grass, out of which rectilinear and circular mowed areas mark the locations of houses and garages. In the largest field, they then called for parallel windbreaks of red pines that cut across the curving streets. Last, a series of fences connects the mowed areas, providing pedestrian connections among the houses.

Salmela and Alt have designed three types of structures: village, prairie, and forest houses. The long, linear village houses have a largely glass first floor containing the main living spaces and a largely solid second floor of bedrooms and baths, with a rooftop terrace. The prairie houses, in contrast, consist of two-story cubes. One cube encloses the living spaces and is connected to a second, bedroom cube by a bridge. Two other cubes, one containing a double garage and the other a studio, join the others to form a foursquare cluster. The forest houses combine elements of the two: a glass-walled living area connected by a second-story bridge to a three-story tower, with a garage on the first floor, two bedrooms and a bath on the second, and a master bedroom suite on the third.

Mayo Woodlands brings to mind a cubist abstraction, and its architecture, the international style, with its nautical references to floating second floors and flying bridges. However, the development also speaks to a new notion of the organic. Rather than present each house and lot as a separate entity, Mayo Woodlands unites all of them into a single, cohesive, "zoological" whole, with windbreaks, fences, and prairie grass disguising property divisions. And rather than cover the landscape in nonnative turf grass that demands much effort and energy to sustain, Mayo Woodlands embraces the "botanical" idea of the organic with its natural growth of native species and its "nautical" architecture open to change over time.

At the same time, the cubist composition of the development provides a dynamic, spatial experience as you drive in and among the rows of windbreaks, and walk in and among the sea of tall grass and the islands of turfgrass. Retaining most of the property in its native state also reduces the time, energy, and resources needed to maintain it, while providing ample accommodation to animal species evicted when the land was farmed. The Mayo family wanted a national model of what a suburb can be, and Coen, Salmela, and Alt have given them that, plus a new and more ecological way of thinking about the organic at a time when we desperately need it.

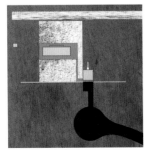
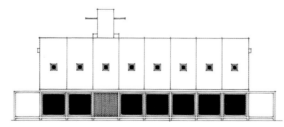
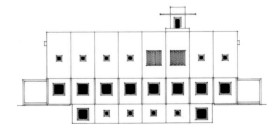

SALMELA'S TYPICAL VILLAGE HOUSE HAS A BEDROOM BLOCK ABOVE AN OPEN, GLASSY GROUND FLOOR.

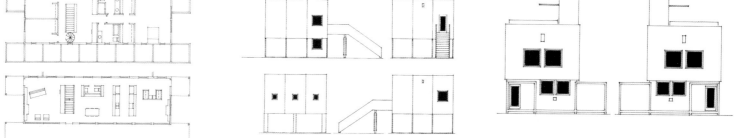

TOP: RECALLING THE SHIP IMAGERY OF EARLY MODERNISM, THE VILLAGE HOUSE SEEMS TO FLOAT ABOVE THE PRAIRIE.

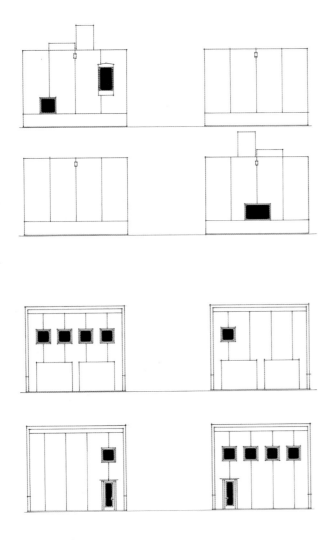

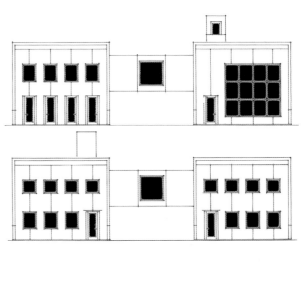

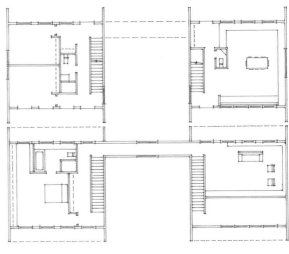

THE PRAIRIE HOUSE HAS TWO GARAGE CUBES AND A HOUSE WITH LINKED LIVING AND SLEEPING CUBES.

THE PRAIRIE HOUSES STAND LIKE MEGALITHS, ROOTED TO THE GROUND, RESISTING THE SWEEP OF GRASS.

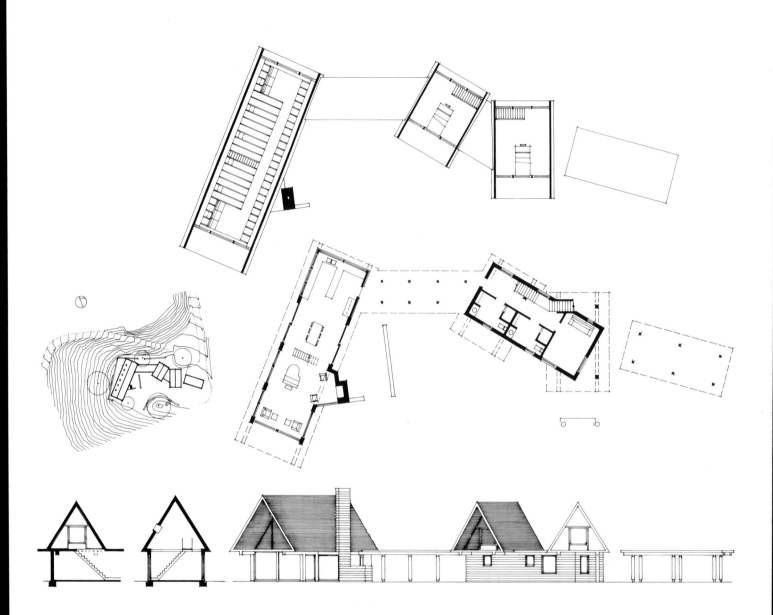

CABIN AND CAMP

THE SETTLING OF THE AMERICAN WEST brought two cultures and economic systems into conflict: the tribal hunting-gathering society of the Native Americans and the capitalistic agricultural-mercantile society of the Europeans. One lived in camps, the other in cabins. While the latter overwhelmed the former, Americans now look back on the settlement of the West and wonder at all that was lost, both culturally and ecologically, with the near annihilation of Native American society, and what could have been learned from those who came before, camping on the land rather than conquering it.

David Salmela's design for the Penhoet house, in the mountains overlooking the California coast, brings that lesson to mind. Replacing an existing house and two cabins on a small plateau partway up the mountain slope, the Penhoet project went through several iterations, gradually becoming less cabinlike and more camplike in its form. The first scheme envisioned a long, narrow house projecting over the edge of the escarpment. It would have had a glass-enclosed main living area, separated by a breezeway from a guesthouse enclosed by glass doors, with two linked, redwood-clad boxes above: one enclosing the master bedroom; the other, guest bedrooms. Roof terraces would have capped both parts of the house.

This design, overtly European in its references to the international style, reflects the westward yearnings of non–Native Americans: the desire to preside over the land and to keep moving until settlers could go no farther. Here, the shiplike references of international style modernism take on new meaning, recalling the "prairie schooners" that Europeans used to cross the sea of grass and that served as their first "houses" upon arrival at the California coast.

As Salmela and the Penhoets continued to work on the design, it evolved in fascinating ways. The house became L-shaped in plan, with a second-story master bedroom above a flat-roofed living area parallel to the slope and a one-story guesthouse with two bedrooms perched on top. The shapes of the second-story bedrooms changed considerably, with curved, faceted, gabled, rectangular, and triangular forms all vying with each other.

The final scheme in some ways recalls Salmela's other work the most. The main house, with its glassy main floor and gabled second level, with an angled chimney pulled out to one side, reminds you of the Emerson house's single gabled-roof living and sleeping room and its angled chimney. Likewise, the two prismlike tubes that serve as guest rooms above a relatively solid base recall the Emerson sauna.

However, those familiar forms take on new meaning here. As the Penhoet house evolved, it became much more camplike, with an open carport and breezeway and tent-like roofs, clustered informally around an open area dominated by the towerlike chimney. The whole looks more like a campground than it does a cabin, which, given what Europeans destroyed in the settlement of the West, might be a fitting form for where their ancestors, remembering those who once roamed this land, might go from here.

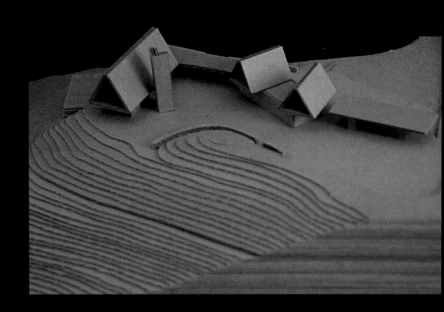

A CARDBOARD MODEL SHOWS THE FINAL DESIGN OF THE PENHOET RETREAT.

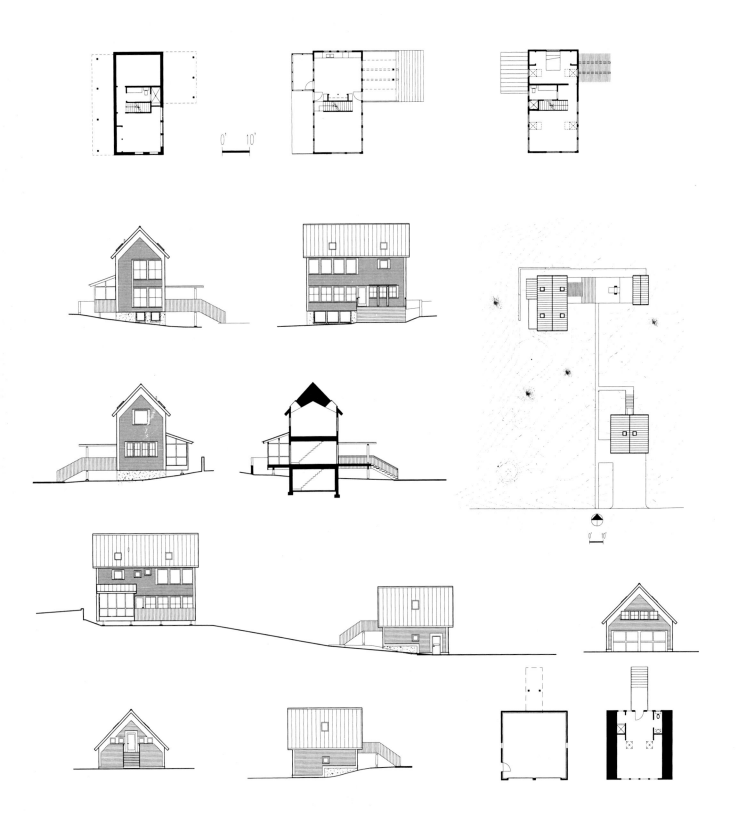

CENTER AND RE-CENTER

OUR HOUSES help us become centered, to feel connected and whole, an ever more important function in a complicated world, where such a feeling becomes increasingly difficult to achieve. It's as if we have to continually recenter ourselves, as implied in this small house for the Andersons by David Salmela.

Salmela has placed at the center of the three-story rectangular house a stair and bathroom core, with a room to either side of it on each floor: a living room and an eat-in kitchen on the main level and two bedrooms on the upper levels. While an efficient plan, this arrangement also seems symbolically loaded: at the center of home, it suggests, we no longer have a gathering place or a hearth, but technology. Yet Salmela, having displaced us from the center of this house, sets about re-centering us on all sides.

He clusters windows and doors asymmetrically within the overall plan of the house, but symmetrically in relation to each other, around smaller centerlines. This small house has at least ten minor symmetries around the three elevations, creating a visual richness unusual for such a modest structure.

Those multiple centers have practical as well as symbolic value. They center us within the various rooms of the house, as if to say that, while no single center holds us anymore, we can still find our bearings in relation to the world, wherever we are. We have only to look for it, at every turn, and this house of many centers shows us how.

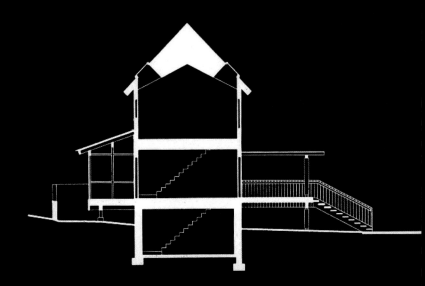

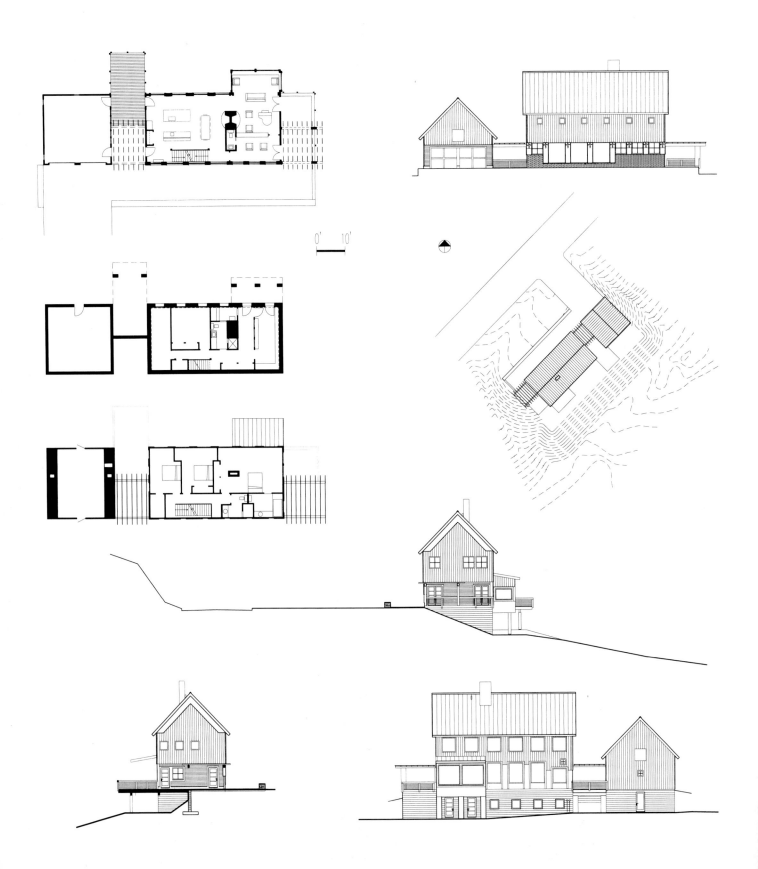

0'   10'

JOGGING

JOGGING has become an American pastime, but it also serves as a theme in architecture, put to good use in this house by David Salmela that overlooks Lake Superior.

To jog means not only to run, but also to push, to remind, to project, or to notch. This house does all of the latter. It and its adjacent garage push up from the sloped site, while the low stone wall along the front yard jogs back from the road, with a swale between them. The house's façade reiterates the idea, with square windows that jog down at the point where the stair descends to the lower level, increasing its illumination.

Elements also jog out from the house: trellises project from its side as well as from between the house and garage, while a deck and a sun porch project from the back of the house, reminding you of the sloped site. The house also jogs our memory. The small clerestory windows along the façade's upper level recall those of local barns, while the continuous line of windows along the first floor, divided by piers with the suggestion of column caps, bring to mind local Arts and Crafts houses.

Inside, the jogging continues. Walls jog to miss windows or capture light, rooms jog to create circulation paths or seating areas, doors jog to line up with each other or with other openings. Many architects avoid such pushing and notching, but when done consistently, as in this house, jogging can be good fun.

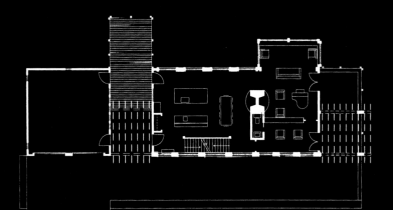

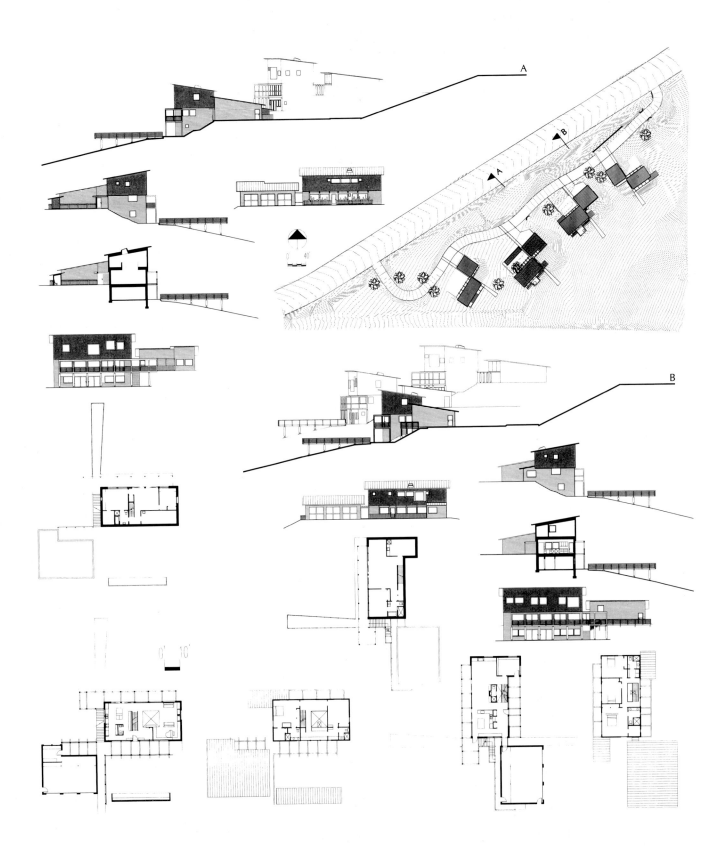

A

B

A

B

0   40'

0'   10'

TYPE AND VARIANT

ANIMALS AND PLANTS develop through variations on a type, and so does architecture. In this development of four houses, David Salmela shows how such a process can lead to considerable architectural invention.

Arrayed along the top of a slope, the four Baumgarten houses all have common features: shed roofs at the same angle and orientation, a projecting garage set off to one side, a trellised porch or deck along the front and back, and a walk, stair, and projecting lookout that create a fracture line between the house and garage. The interior arrangements also have the main rooms facing the view of Lake Superior to the south and utility spaces along the north.

Within those common themes, Salmela plays several variations. One house has two bedrooms upstairs, with a large, two-story space connecting to the main living floor; another has three upstairs bedrooms, with a narrow slot of space to the floor below. One house has a music alcove; another, a main-floor office accessible directly from the front porch. One has a front lawn; another, a front court screened from the street by a shed-roofed bench enclosure.

Housing developers, of course, have long played the game of superficial variations of standard plans. But this development differs in fundamental ways: the plans are anything but standard, the variations anything but superficial. As such, it represents not just a variation, but also a real evolution.

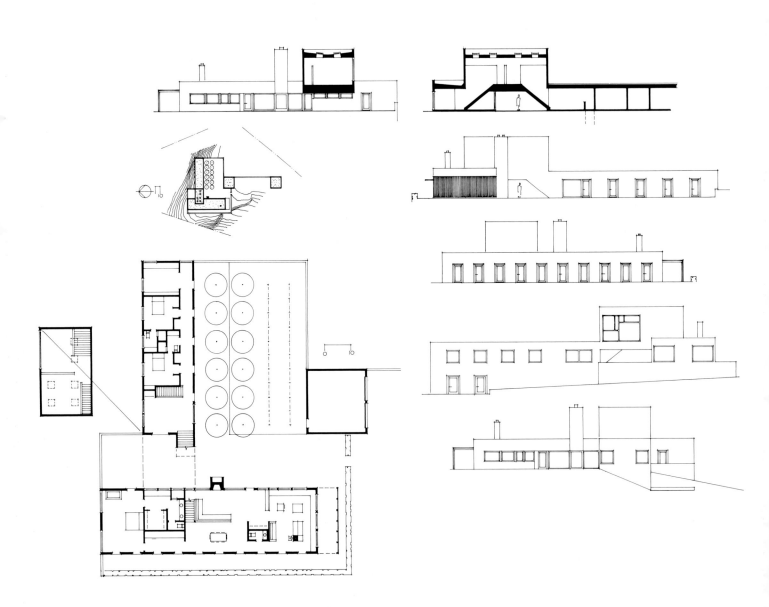

APART AND ∧ PART

ALL ART, to varying degrees, is both a part of and apart from daily life, responding to what surrounds us and transcends us at the same time. David Salmela's Bolen house gives form to that idea.

The house has two separate perpendicular structures: one contains the main living spaces such as the kitchen, dining and living area, and master bedroom; the other, two additional bedrooms and living and working spaces. An art studio bridges these wings. The studio features a large, asymmetrically divided, north-facing window; six skylights hidden behind a parapet; and stairs of different widths giving access to both wings. Under the studio bridge runs a terrace that extends from the car court, with its pair of double garages, past an enclosed garden and an arbor of trees to a view at the north end of the house.

The art studio does not just bridge the two parts of the house functionally; it also provides a visual and sym-bolic link. With its angled stair enclosure, the studio seems to reach out and over the main house. At the same time, the mostly blank walls of the studio provide a counterpoint to the regular rhythms of glass doors and windows of the two wings. Here, art is a part of and apart from the house and garden, connected to the activities of daily life and rising above them—just where art should be.

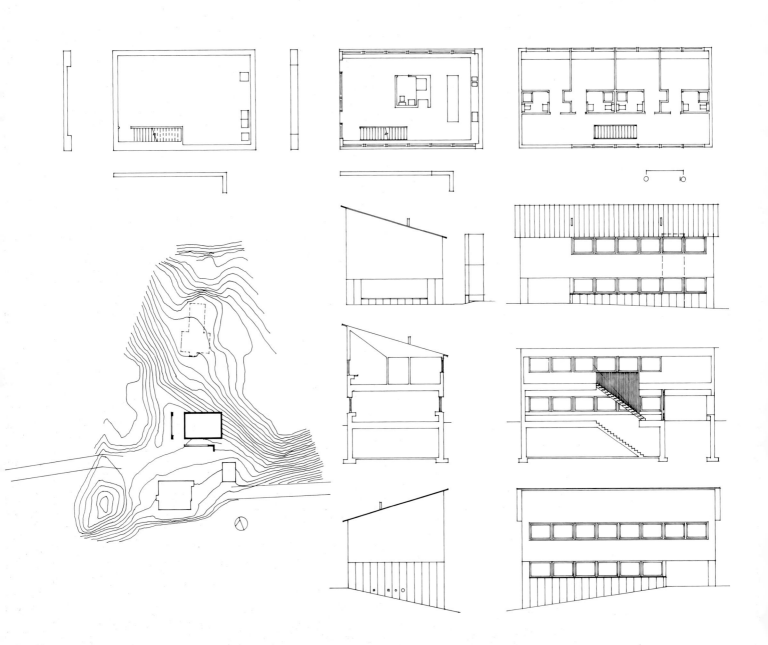

COMMON HOUSE

ALVAR AALTO, in several of his dormitories, called for shared living spaces and widened hallways next to stairs to get individuals out of their private rooms to engage in what he called "social-collective living." This small dormitory for interns at the Cable Natural History Museum, which David Salmela worked on with Vincent James and Associates, recalls that aspect of Aalto's work.

The intern housing has four private rooms on the upper floor, each with a sloped ceiling, a closet, and a bathroom, and all facing a wide corridor with a stair at its center. On the main floor, a common living, eating, and kitchen area has a central bathroom core and almost continuous glazing on three sides. A terrace, covered by the extension of the floor above, provides outdoor living space for the interns as well. Utilities, laundry equipment, and storage space occupy the partial basement.

The emphasis on collective living here has become uncommon, even in dormitories, in part because the word "common" has taken on such negative connotations. We often think of the word not only referring to what we share, but also to what we might consider ordinary or of low quality. Privacy, which shares its root word with privation, has in turn, become what we most prize. This intern housing refutes that trend. It shows how common space can set a place apart and enhance a sense of community, all within a building whose simple, elegant form is anything but ordinary. Would that we had more buildings like this in common.

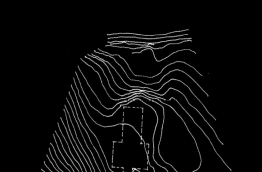

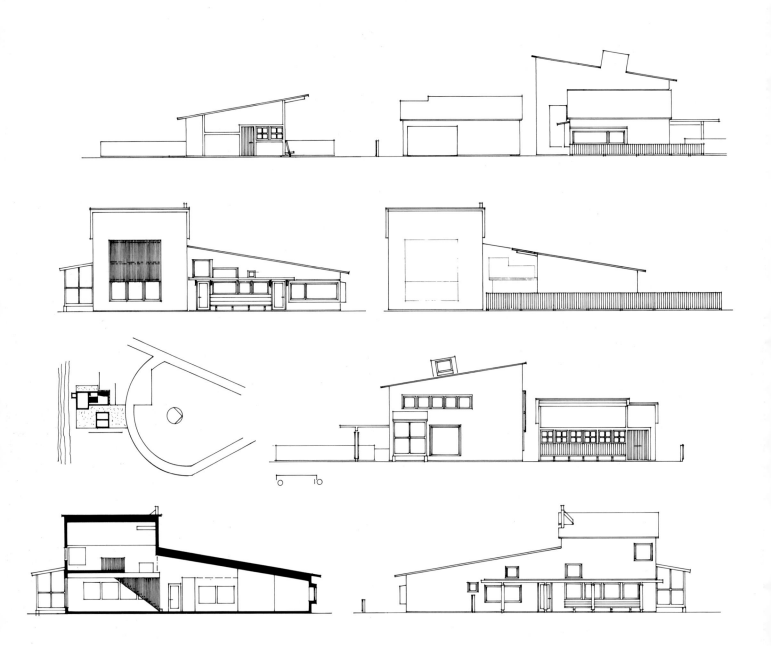

tive. Over the last century, we also discovered the tricks that perspective can play on us, evident in the Chelsey art studio by David Salmela.

One such trick is the foreshortening of our perspective, as Salmela performs here with the long shed roof of the studio, which makes it look shorter from the exterior and either shorter or longer on the interior, depending upon which way you look. Another trick involves causing one thing to look like something else from a particular vantage point. What looks like a tilting chimney along the slope of the second-story shed roof is, in fact, the back of a skylight that illuminates the studio below.

Differences of size also suggest depth in perspective where it doesn't exist. Salmela uses windows of varying size and height in this studio to imply a degree of depth in an otherwise flat wall. The diversity of windows also helps to frame differing views of the outside, suggesting that our own perspective as we move through space can profoundly change our perspective on the world. That idea—the relativity and variability of perspective—has set twentieth-century art apart from what preceded it, and it certainly sets this studio apart as a work of architecture.

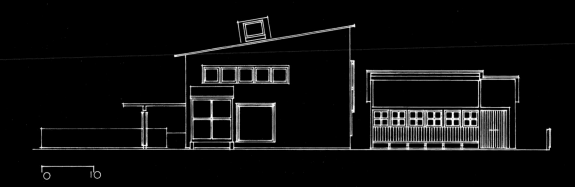

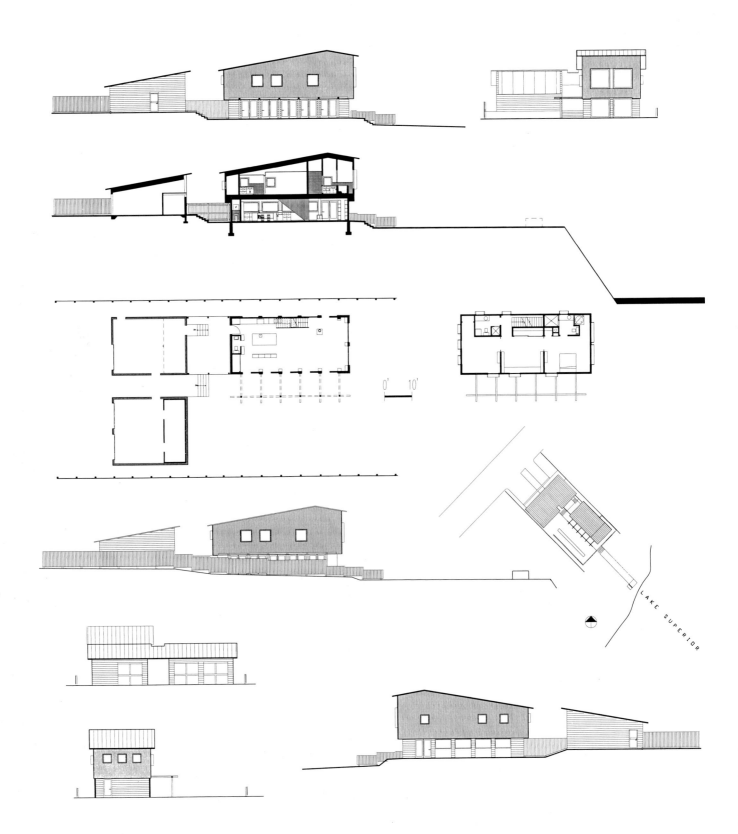

LAKE SUPERIOR

STREAMLINED NATURE

BUILDINGS RARELY MOVE, and yet over the last one hundred years, "streamlined" architecture has tried to create a sense of movement. As we have become more mobile, we have wanted our structures to appear so as well, and David Salmela's Cotruvo house offers an unconventional way of looking at that phenomenon.

The house and its pair of garages have shed roofs of the same slope and plane, creating a streamlined form that looks as if it were shaped by the wind off Lake Superior. At the same time, the breezeway, which divides the two garages, has the quality of being carved out of a mass, as if through erosion. These forms suggest movement, although not that of a machine, which characterized early modern architecture, but that of nature's scouring action, appropriate here on the shore of a Great Lake.

Inside the house, the movement of nature takes a different form. Here, it is the wind itself that moves through the largely open main kitchen, dining, and living area, whose glass doors and large windows wrap three sides of this floor, allowing for ample cross-ventilation. Upstairs, large openings between the master bedroom and guest room, and large windows on all sides, allow for the movement of space and air, emphasized with the upward slope of the ceiling.

The idea of streamlining began with our emulation of the machine, but it may be that the streamlining of nature affected by the wind provides a more environmentally appropriate symbol for our own time.

CABIN CULTURE

IN MINNESOTA, many people have small cabins by one of the state's thousands of lakes, primitive huts to which you can escape the pressures of modern life. The Driscoll cabin represents that aspect of Minnesota culture and exaggerates the traits that have made lakeside cottages so popular.

The rectilinear cabin has a central stair dividing the first-floor living and master bedroom from the dining room, kitchen, and bath/mudroom. On the second floor, the stair separates two bedrooms tucked under the steep gable roof. The front of the cabin has a central door and two small square windows; the back facing the lake, a row of large square windows with a central door leading to a partly covered deck.

The simplicity of the plan contrasts with the expression of the elevations. The front and back exterior walls lean out, as if pushed by the steep gable roof that rests upon them. Vertical board-and-batten siding accentuates that outward tilt and alludes to the cottagelike scale of the structure. An arch-topped bench, a gable-roofed porch, and a broad flight of stairs down from the deck all add to the quality of informality and leisure associated with cabin culture.

This cabin has yet another quality: that of fantasy. Like a child's drawing of a cabin, in which nothing is quite straight or totally serious, the Driscolls' weekend and summer retreat reminds us that we go to the lake not only to forget the pressures of adulthood, but also to remember the pleasures of childhood.

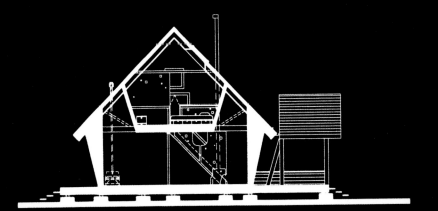

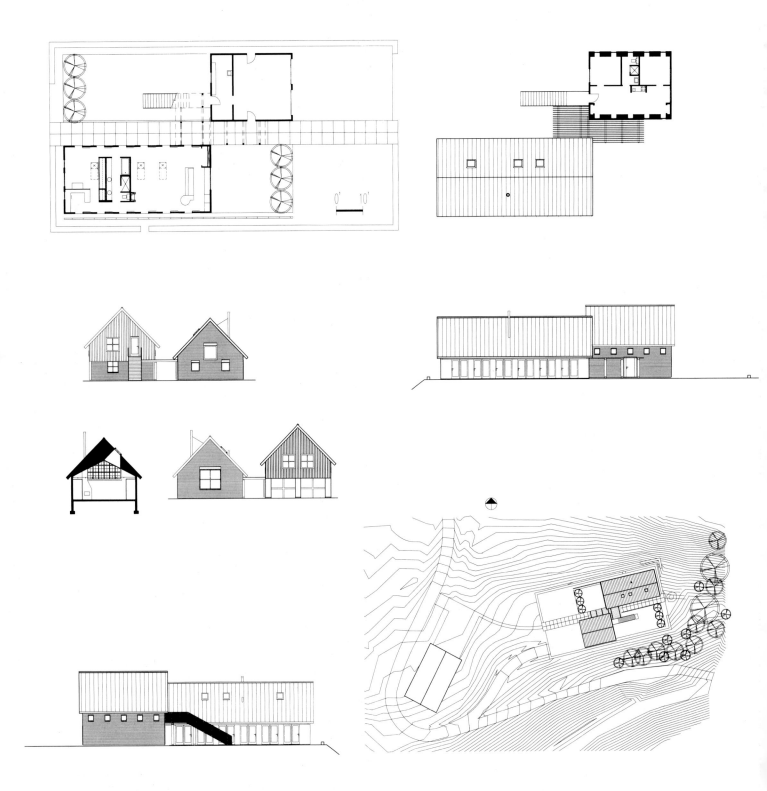

0'   10'

MAJOR AND MINOR

WE TYPICALLY ORGANIZE our lives into major and minor activities, giving some things priority over others. Architects do the same thing in buildings, even though, as David Salmela suggests in the Gernander-Burke house, we need to question those priorities at the same time.

The house consists of a single room, with a bathroom core dividing the master bedroom and study from the living, dining, and kitchen area. A trellis-covered walk, which extends down the middle of the yard from front to back, separates the house from a two-car garage, with a two-bedroom studio apartment above, accessed via a stair off the back. In plan, the two structures seem perfectly paired. The garage looks as if it had flipped to the other side of the walk, vacating a space that became the front yard of the house and creating privacy for the backyard. Visually, the two also complement each other. Both structures have the same roof pitch and material, and the same overall form.

And yet other features raise doubts about the hierarchy of the two buildings. While functionally secondary to the house, the garage stands farther forward, is taller, and has greater solidity. Meanwhile the house, functionally more central, has a considerable setback, an uncertain scale given its large front window, and a pavilionlike character with walls of glass doors. The plans of the two buildings—a traditional room plan for the garage's apartment versus a modernist "free" plan for the house—suggest that major and minor elements can flip, that priorities do not always remain stable, and that the acceptance of difference in our complex lives may be a better strategy than the imposition of hierarchies that may not hold.

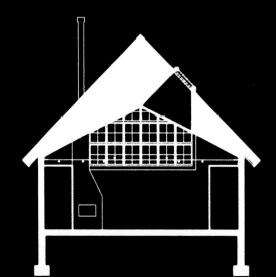

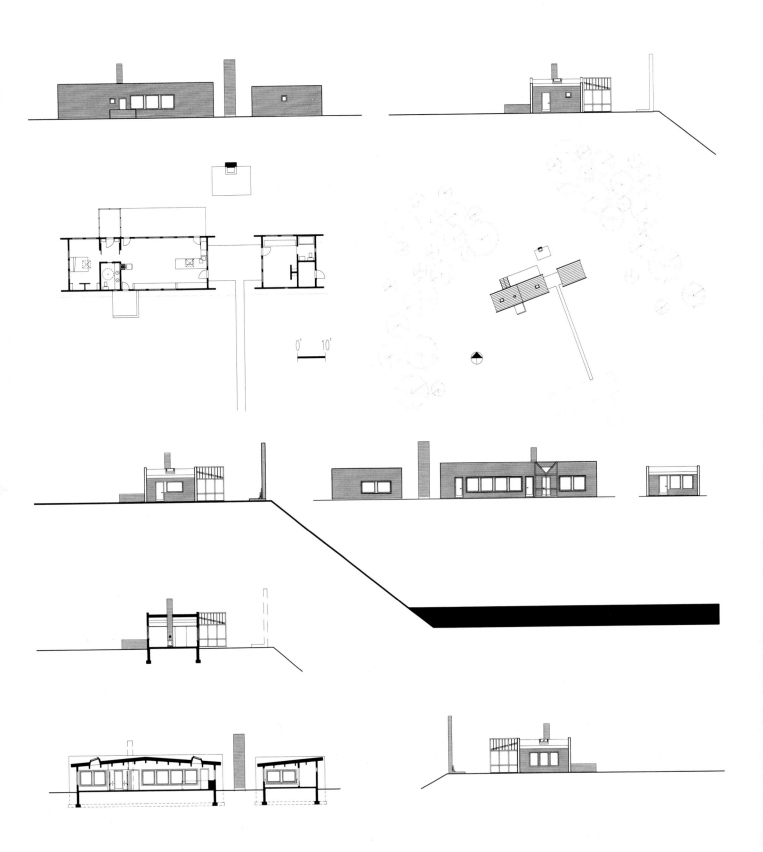

0'   10'

WATER AND FALL

HUMANS HAVE LONG SOUGHT to settle by the sea, be it for proximity to food or convenience of transportation or, more recently, for rest and relaxation. Securing shelter by the sea, though, can be difficult, as the Golob-Freeman cabin David Salmela has designed on Madeline Island in Lake Superior attests.

The long, rectangular building has one bedroom, a bathroom, and a kitchen, dining, and living area all in one space. A patio, with an adjacent outdoor fireplace, separates the main house from the guest quarters with its own bathroom. These two small structures seem dwarfed by the wilderness that surrounds them, and so Salmela has, with the simplest of means, secured a sense of shelter.

He does this first by extending the exterior side walls beyond the corners and above the low-sloped roofs. These walls protect the wood-framed structure within while facing right into the north wind. Salmela has also had the exterior walls painted black. Although unusual, the cabin's black exterior contrasts with the white interior and red ceiling, creating a sense of psychological safety, a warm, white place in a cold, dark world. And, as if to stare nature in the face, Salmela has put a lightly framed screened porch outside the wall, with a butterfly roof to shed the rain, like a big scupper, spouting water back to the lake below. The wall is not only there because of the water of the lake below, but that water, in some small way, is there because of the wall and what it supports and protects.

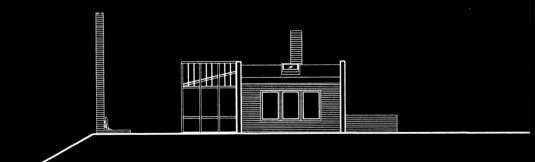

ARCHITECTURE can draw upon language as much as literature, although rarely with the degree of wit that you find in David Salmela's design of the Keel cabin, which seems to draw upon the owner's name.

The most striking feature of the cabin is its gable roof, which extends straight over the main part of the house, then slopes down to the adjacent bunkhouse and back up again. It looks as if a nearby tree had keeled over, permanently denting the roof ridge. Inside the cabin, the exposed trusses reinforce a reading of the roof as an overturned hull, with its ridge now a broken keel.

This wordplay continues on the elevations. The plan of the cabin is simple, with a kitchen, dining room, living room, and porch on the first floor, a master bedroom and extra beds on the second floor and in the bunkhouse. But Salmela has designed the elevations with as diverse a fenestration as possible. Windows of all shapes and sizes— large and small, curved and straight, high and low—jostle for space on the exterior walls, as if trying to regain an even keel. While each opening has a purpose, a particular space to light or view to provide, you do feel as if the house had been keelhauled out of a window factory, with one of every kind of unit on it.

Architecture doesn't write or speak, but it can make language three-dimensional and spatial, waiting for you to discover it, to find your own keel.

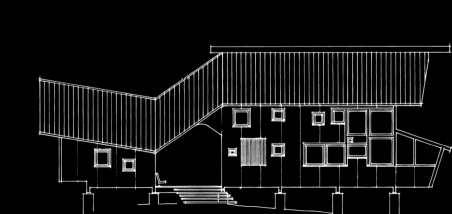

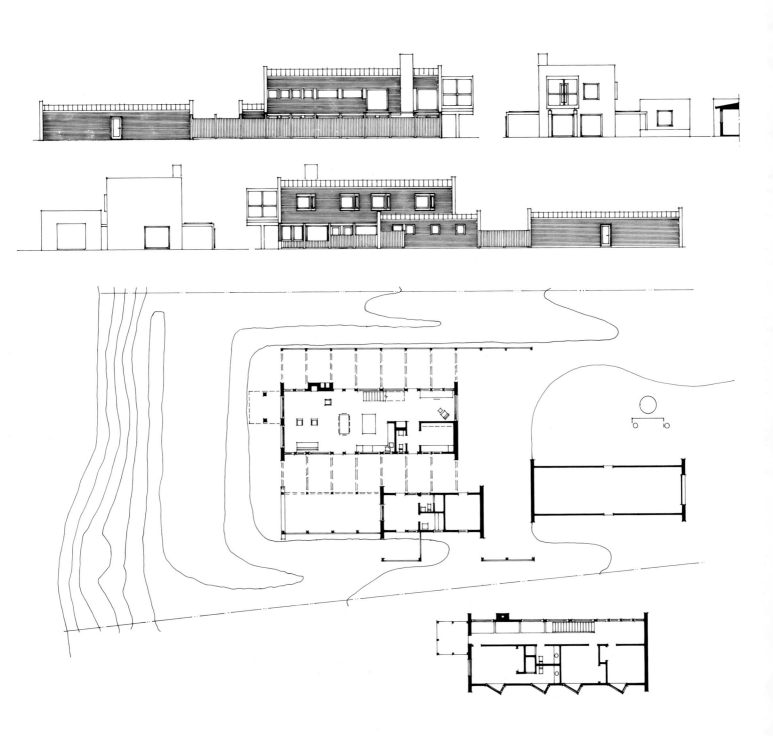

Matthew cabin by David Salmela brings those two types of layering together.

The lakeside compound includes a long, narrow two-car garage; a separate sauna and storage building; and a two-story, three-bedroom main house, each of which consists of a series of vertical and horizontal layers. Each structure has a front and back wall that extends beyond the edge of the building and above the low-sloped roof, as if part of a series of vertical layers across the property. Side fences and trellises that extend along either side of the complex reinforce that idea.

Inside the house, the layering continues. An entry zone, with front and back doors facing each other on either side of the house, leads to an office and work zone to one side and a zone of service functions (bathroom, kitchen, stair) to the other. A living and dining room occupies the layer that looks over the lake. Upstairs, the bedrooms and bathrooms have a similar layering, with a circulation zone culminating in a second-floor screened porch.

Layering the house and landscape in this way not only provides a clear organization to a disparate group of structures, but also reminds us of the layers of our own lives, played out as we move along or across the layers of the world.

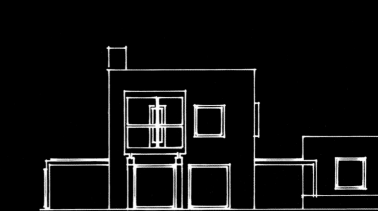

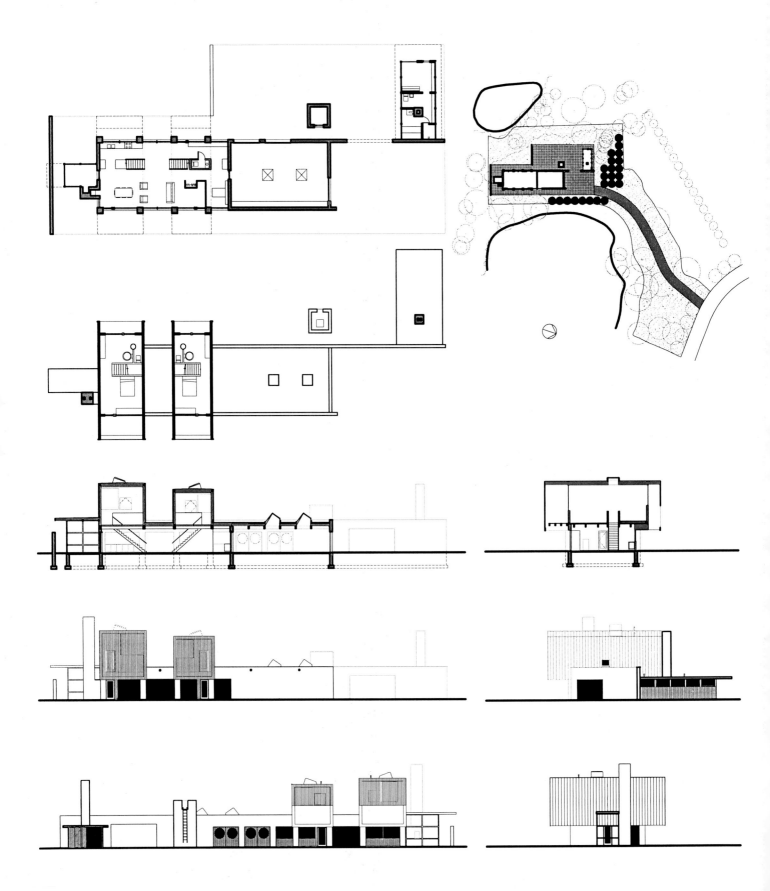

THE MODERN BOX

MODERN ARCHITECTS, despite their many differences, have largely shared in the desire to break out of the box, as Frank Lloyd Wright put it—to open corners, expand space, and generally break free of the tradition of discreet, boxlike rooms. David Salmela, in the Streeter house, challenges that idea. He has designed a thoroughly modern house and yet, at the same time, has played up its boxlike appearance.

Approaching the house from the drive, you come upon a wall with two openings, one of glass illuminating the garage behind and the other open to a walk that leads you to the front door midway along the side of the house. A boxlike structure cantilevers out over the entry; open on the end, it has nearly blank side walls. This box stands next to another slightly taller and wider box, which also projects perpendicular to the main floor.

Inside the house, living, dining, and kitchen areas occupy the glassy back half of the main floor, with a garage and office in the front half. Between the kitchen and living areas, two facing stairs ascend in opposite directions to the two boxes above, each of which contains a bedroom, bathroom, closet, and deck screened by narrow, vertical slats. To emphasize the point, Salmela has boxlike enclosures around the bedrooms' side windows as well as the skylight bringing light to the floor below.

The Streeter house makes you wonder if breaking out of the box is key to modern architecture or if it has become a phase we needed to go through to rediscover the box for new purposes and in a new vocabulary of forms—as Salmela has here.

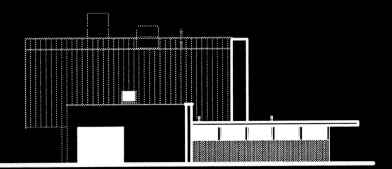

NEW AND OLD

LIFE IS A CONSTANT PROCESS of rehabilitation, of making internal changes and external additions to what already exists. In the Tofte-Broberg cottage, David Salmela gives that process a particularly lively form.

Starting with an existing structure, Salmela both restored and altered it. The house has a central line of stairs, one leading to a second-floor office/bedroom and another leading to a walkout basement. A living area occupies one end of the main floor, a master-bedroom suite the other end, with a sky-lit kitchen on one side opening to a glassy dining room overlooking Prairie Lake. Salmela has also added a glassed-in entry vestibule and porch a couple of steps above the main cottage floor.

The gable roofs express the changes to the cottage over time, with steeper roof slopes at the center leading to a variety of shallower slopes along the eaves. The three-car garage echoes that idea, with a cluster of three gables over the front of the building and a single shed roof over the back.

The variety of roof slopes, along with the diversity of window sizes and siding types on this cottage, conveys the informality of lakeside living. But they also suggest something else. Architecture, like life itself, doesn't have complete coherence as it changes, grows, and adapts over time. Nevertheless, we can learn to appreciate and even love its inconsistencies. This cottage, with all of its changes and additions, gives us plenty of opportunities to do just that.

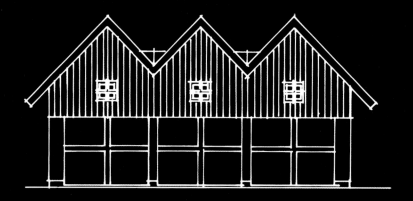

BUILDING | CREDITS

BRANDENBURG'S RAVENWOOD STUDIO
Owners: Jim and Judy Brandenburg
Location: Ely, Minnesota
Date designed: 1995
Architect: Salmela Architect. (initiated under Salmela
Fosdick, Ltd.)
Structural engineers: Hurst and Henrichs, Ltd.,
and Carroll, Franck, and Associates
Contractor: Rod and Sons Carpentry
Masonry contractor: L and K Masonry

EMERSON RESIDENCE AND SAUNA
Owners: Peter and Cynthia Emerson
Location: Cooke Lake, Duluth, Minnesota
Date designed: 1997–2002
Architect: Salmela Architect. (initiated under Salmela Fosdick, Ltd.)
Landscape architect: Coen + Stumpf and Associates
Structural engineer: Kreck and Ojard
Contractor: Rod and Sons Carpentry

WILD RICE RESTAURANT
Owner: Mary Rice
Location: Bayfield, Wisconsin
Date designed: 2000
Architect: Salmela Architect
(David Salmela and Souliyahn Keobounpheng)
Landscape architect: Coen + Stumpf and Associates
Structural engineer: Hurst and Henrichs, Ltd.
Contractor: Wayne Nassi Construction

ALBRECHT RESIDENCE
Owners: Arlin and Marilyn Albrecht
Location: Red Wing, Minnesota
Date designed: 1999
Architect: Salmela Architect
(David Salmela and Souliyahn Keobounpheng)
Landscape architect: Coen + Stumpf and Associates
Colorist: Carol Stumpf
Furniture consultant: Janet Sawyer
Contractors: Alms Construction and River City Builders

SCOTT-KERZE CABIN AND SAUNA
Owner: Peter Bastianelli-Kerze
Location: St. Mary's Lake, Eveleth, Minnesota
Date designed: 1979–2000
Architect: Salmela Architect (David Salmela and Peter Kerze).
Initiated through Damberg, Scott, Peck, and Booker.
Contractors: Gary Makela Construction and Peter Kerze

JACKSON MEADOW
Developers: Harold Teasdale and Robert Durfey
Location: Marine on St. Croix, Minnesota
Date designed: 1998
Architects and landscape architects: Salmela Architect,
Coen + Stumpf and Associates, and Coen + Partners
(David Salmela, Jon Stumpf, Shane Coen, Souliyahn
Keobounpheng, Nathan Anderson, Travis Van Liere,
Stephanie Grotta, and Bryan Kramer)
Structural engineer: Carroll, Franck, and Associates
Colorist: Carol Stumpf
Wetland engineering: RLK Engineers
Contractors: Cates Construction and Anderson Sorenson Homes

JONES FARMSTEAD
Owners: Douglas and Mary Jones
Location: Nerstrand, Minnesota
Date designed: 1997
Architect: Salmela Architect
(David Salmela and Souliyahn Keobounpheng)
Landscape architect: Coen + Stumpf and Associates
Structural engineer: Carroll, Franck, and Associates
Contractor: River City Builders

KOEHLER RETREAT
Owners: Tom and Stephanie Koehler
Location: Silver Bay, Minnesota
Date designed: 2000
Architect: Salmela Architect
(David Salmela and Souliyahn Keobounpheng)
Landscape architect: Coen + Stumpf and Associates
Structural engineer: Carroll, Franck, and Associates
Contractor: Rod and Sons Carpentry

GOOSEBERRY FALLS STATE PARK VISITORS CENTER
Owner: State of Minnesota
Location: Two Harbors, Minnesota
Date designed: 1992
Architect: Salmela Fosdick, Ltd. (David Salmela, principal,
and Cheryl Fosdick). Finished through Salmela Architect.
Landscape architect: Coen + Stumpf and Associates
Civil engineer: LHB Engineers and Architects
Structural engineer: Hurst and Henrichs, Ltd.
Mechanical engineer: Gausman and Moore
Contractor: Rueben Johnson and Sons

SMITH RESIDENCE
Owners: Brian and Tia Smith
Location: Lakeville, Minnesota
Date designed: 1990
Architect: Salmela Fosdick, Ltd. (David Salmela)
Contractor: Widlund Construction

LOKEN RESIDENCE
Owners: Cal and Amy Loken
Location: Duluth, Minnesota
Date designed: 1990
Architect: Salmela Fosdick, Ltd. (David Salmela)
Contractor: Rod and Sons Carpentry

HANSON RETREAT
Owners: Jay and Madge Hanson
Location: Gunflint Trail, Grand Marais, Minnesota
Date designed: 1992
Architect: Salmela Fosdick, Ltd. (David Salmela)
Contractor: Lande Construction

LUTZ RESIDENCE
Owners: Paul and Dorothy Lutz
Location: Pike Lake, Duluth, Minnesota
Date designed: 1993
Architect: Salmela Fosdick, Ltd. (David Salmela)
Contractor: Rod and Sons Carpentry

CARLSON RESIDENCE AND OUTBUILDINGS
Owners: Mark and Mary Dell Carlson
RESIDENCE
Location: Duluth, Minnesota
Date designed: 1998
Architect: Salmela Architect
Landscape architect: Coen + Stumpf and Associates
Contractor: Rod and Sons Carpentry
OUTBUILDINGS
Location: Lake Nebagamon, Wisconsin
Date designed: 1994
Architect: Salmela Architect
Contractor: Jerry Martinson

WEBSTER RESIDENCE
Owners: Keith and Jane Webster
Location: Lake Eshquagama, Biwabik, Minnesota
Date designed: 1979
Architect: David Salmela, while with Damberg, Scott, Peck, and Booker
Contractor: Gary Makela Construction

WICK STUDIO AND RESIDENCE
Owners: Mel and Faith Wick
Location: Cohasset, Minnesota
Date designed: 1979
Architect: David Salmela, while with Damberg, Scott, Peck, and Booker
Contractor: Seipp Construction

THOMPSON RESIDENCE
Owners: Richard and Phyllis Thompson
Location: Grand Rapids, Minnesota
Date designed: 1987
Architect: David Salmela, while with Damberg, Scott, Peck, and Booker
Contractor: Rod and Sons Carpentry

UNGER-SONNERUP RESIDENCE
Owners: Paul Unger and Kirsten Sonnerup
Location: Charlotte, Vermont
Date designed: 1996
Architect: Salmela Architect
Structural engineers: Carroll, Franck, and Associates
Contractor: Roundtree Construction

MORA VASALOPPET NORDIC SKI CENTER
Location: Mora, Minnesota
Date designed: 2000
Architect: Salmela Architect
(David Salmela and Souliyahn Keobounpheng)
Contractor: Benji Krawiecki Construction

HOLMES FARMSTEAD
Owners: Rod and Joan Holmes
Location: Aurora, Minnesota
Date designed: 1995
Architect: Salmela Architect (initiated under Salmela Fosdick, Ltd.)
Contractor: Rod and Sons Carpentry

HOLMES RESIDENCE
Owners: Bradley and Kristine Holmes
Location: Gilbert, Minnesota
Date designed: 1994
Architect: Salmela Architect
Contractor: Rod and Sons Carpentry

LEAKE WORKSHOP
Owners: Donald and Sandra Leake
Location: Duluth, Minnesota
Date designed: 1993
Architect: Salmela Fosdick, Ltd. (David Salmela, design principal)
Contractor: Ericson Construction

AAS RESIDENCE
Owners: Hans and Martha Aas
Location: Duluth, Minnesota
Date designed: 1991
Architect: Salmela Fosdick, Ltd.
(David Salmela, design principal, and Cheryl Fosdick)
Contractor: Builders Commonwealth

SALMELA RESIDENCE
Owners: Lyle and Elaine Salmela
Location: Arden Hills, Minnesota
Date designed: 1991
Architect: Salmela Fosdick, Ltd. (David Salmela)
Contractor: Blaine Construction

WILSON RESIDENCE
Owners: Robert and Joan Wilson
Location: Lake Vermilion, Tower, Minnesota
Date designed: 1989
Architect: Salmela Fosdick, Ltd. (David Salmela)
Contractor: Rod and Sons Carpentry

MAYO WOODLANDS
Owner and developer: Mayo Family
Location: Rochester, Minnesota
Date designed: 2001 (in design)
Prime consultant: Coen + Partners (Shane Coen, Nathan Anderson, Travis Van Liere, Stephanie Grotta, Bryan Kramer)
Architects: Altus Architect, Ltd. (Tim Alt, Roger Angaran, Chad Healy, Patrick Freet, and Carl Olson) and Salmela Architect (David Salmela and Souliyahn Keobounpheng)
Contractor: Thomas Bren Homes

PENHOET RETREAT
Owners: Edward and Camille Penhoet
Location: Big Sur, California
Date designed: 2001 (in design)
Architect: Salmela Architect (David Salmela, Souliyahn Keobounpheng, Tia Salmela Keobounpheng)
Associate architect: Flescher and Foster

ANDERSON RESIDENCE
Owners: John and Mary Anderson
Location: Bayfield, Wisconsin
Date designed: 2001
Architect: Salmela Architect
(David Salmela and Souliyahn Keobounpheng)
Landscape architect: Coen + Partners
Contractor: Bayfield Construction

ARVOLD RESIDENCE
Owners: David and Judith Arvold
Location: Duluth, Minnesota
Date designed: 2001
Architect: Salmela Architect
(David Salmela and Souliyahn Keobounpheng)
Landscape architect: Coen + Partners
Contractors: Rod and Sons Carpentry, Johnston Masonry, Hedberg Excavation, Heating Plus

BAUMGARTEN DEVELOPMENT
Owners: John and Kathy Baumgarten and Joe and Susan Dusek
Location: Duluth, Minnesota
Date designed: 2002
Architect: Salmela Architect
(David Salmela and Souliyahn Keobounpheng)
Landscape architect: Coen + Partners
Structural engineer: Carroll, Franck, and Associates
Contractors: Rod and Sons Carpentry, Johnston Masonry, Hedberg Excavation, Heating Plus

BOLEN RESIDENCE
Owners: Michael and Betsy Bolen
Location: Kirkwood, Missouri
Date designed: 2002 (in design)
Architect: Salmela Architect (David Salmela, Souliyahn Keobounpheng, Scott Muellner, and Carly Coulson)
Landscape architect: Coen + Partners

CABLE NATURAL HISTORY MUSEUM INTERN HOUSING
Owner: Cable Natural History Museum
Location: Cable, Wisconsin
Date designed: 2000
Architects: Joint venture by Vince James Associates and Salmela Architect (Vince James and David Salmela, principals; Nathan Knutson, project architect; and Tia Salmela Keobounpheng)
Contractor: Wayne Nassi Construction

CHESLEY STUDIO

Owner: Margaret Chesley
Location: Bay City, Wisconsin
Date designed: 1996
Architect: Salmela Architect
Landscape architect: Coen + Stumpf and Associates
Contractor: River City Builders

COTRUVO RESIDENCE

Owners: Thomas and Christina Cotruvo
Location: Duluth, Minnesota
Date designed: 2001
Architect: Salmela Architect
(David Salmela and Souliyahn Keobounpheng)
Landscape architect: Coen + Partners
Structural engineer: Carroll, Franck, and Associates
Contractors: Rod and Sons Carpentry, Johnston Masonry,
Hedberg Excavation

DRISCOLL CABIN

Owners: Todd and Cynthia Driscoll
Location: Lake Vermilion, Soudan, Minnesota
Date designed: 2001
Architect: Salmela Architect
(David Salmela and Souliyahn Keobounpheng)
Contractor: Rod and Sons Carpentry

GERNANDER-BURKE RESIDENCE

Owners: Kent Gernander and Elizabeth Burke
Location: Winona, Minnesota
Date designed: 2001
Architect: Salmela Architect
(David Salmela and Souliyahn Keobounpheng)
Landscape architect: Coen + Partners
Contractor: Roemer Construction

GOLOB-FREEMAN CABIN

Owners: Bruce Golob and Jean Freeman
Location: Madeline Island, La Pointe, Wisconsin
Date designed: 2000
Architect: Salmela Architect
(David Salmela and Souliyahn Keobounpheng)
Landscape architect: Coen + Partners
Structural engineer: Carroll, Franck, and Associates
Contractor: Northwoods Construction

KEEL CABIN

Owners: Karl and Mary Keel
Location: White Face Reservoir, St. Louis County, Minnesota
Date designed: 2001
Architect: Salmela Architect
(David Salmela and Souliyahn Keobounpheng)
Contractor: Rod and Sons Carpentry

MATTHEW CABIN

Owners: David and Kathy Matthew
Location: Gull Lake, Brainerd, Minnesota
Date designed: 2002
Architect: Salmela Architect
(David Salmela, Souliyahn Keobounpheng, and Jon Lintula)
Landscape architect: Coen + Partners
Contractor: Majka Construction

STREETER RESIDENCE

Owner: Kevin Streeter
Location: Greenwood, Minnesota
Date designed: 2002
Architect: Salmela Architect
(David Salmela, Souliyahn Keobounpheng, Scott Muellner,
and Carly Coulson)
Landscape architect: Coen + Partners
Structural engineer: Carroll, Franck, and Associates

TOFTE-BROBERG COTTAGE

Owners: David Broberg and Jacquelyn Tofte
Location: Grand Rapids, Minnesota
Date designed: 1999
Architect: Salmela Architect
Contractors: Brian Kuntio and Greg Stone

THOMAS FISHER is dean of the College of Architecture and Landscape Architecture at the University of Minnesota. He is a contributing editor of *Architecture Magazine* and previously served as the editorial director of *Progressive Architecture Magazine*. He is the author of *In the Scheme of Things: Alternative Thinking on the Practice of Architecture*, published by the University of Minnesota Press.

DAVID SALMELA, FAIA, is the principal architect in the firm Salmela Architect in Duluth, Minnesota. Since 1987, his projects have won fourteen Minnesota American Institute of Architects Honor Awards and fourteen national level awards, including a National AIA Honor Award for Architecture for his design of Jim Brandenburg's Ravenwood Studio in Ely, Minnesota.

PETER BASTIANELLI-KERZE's architectural photographs have appeared in more than a dozen books published in the United States, England, Germany, Spain, Italy, and Japan. They have also been published in numerous magazines, such as *Abitare, A+U, Architecture, Architectural Record, Architectural Review, El Croquis, Graphis, Hauser,* and *Wood Design and Building*. He has been honored for his exceptional photography by the Minnesota AIA.